MUSIC CITY BLUES

FROM THE TRAINING ACADEMY TO THE STREETS... A GLIMPSE AT WHAT LIFE BEHIND THE BADGE IS *REALLY LIKE*

By Scott Fielden

Based on the accounts of Officer Mark Fielden, M.N.P.D.

printed by
The Overmountain Press
325 W. Walnut St.
Johnson City, TN 37604

THE VIEWS EXPRESSED HEREIN DO NOT NECESSARILY REFLECT THE POLICIES AND PROCEDURES OF THE NASHVILLE METROPOLITIAN POLICE DEPARTMENT

Seventy-two police officers
were killed by gunfire in 1993,
more than half of all those who
have died in the line of duty.
A total of 2,278 shooting deaths
of law enforcement officers have
occurred since 1960.

-National Association of Chiefs of Police

TABLE OF CONTENTS

INTRODUCTION

For those who prefer to consume a "meat and potatoes" literary diet, I hope you'll take a minute to enjoy the following appetizer before moving straight to dinner, as this section is reserved for a moment of retrospect, a time to reflect upon the five years that my brother, Mark Fielden, and I spent collaborating on this book.

During this period, I had the unique opportunity to peer behind the semi-closed doors surrounding the life of police officers. And throughout this "learning" experience, one word continuously came to mind as I settled down in front of my word processor, obsessed with somehow bringing alive the emotions buried deep within the mountain of notes I had compiled.

Unique. That's perhaps the best pair of syllables to describe what it's like to be a cop.

It takes a special breed of people to devote their lives to law enforcement. After all, they're constantly fighting a war they *can't possibly win*. But thankfully, for the rest of us, they have the courage and insight to know that if no resistance is given, then the other side triumphs without a struggle.

And should that ever happen, we all will lose.

I fondly recall as a child spending many carefree summer afternoons vigorously playing "cops and robbers" with my older brother, Mark. The air in our yard was constantly filled with the sounds and lingering powder scents from our Woolworth's metal cap pistols as we acted out our childhood fantasies with the energy and enthusiasm of a Broadway play during opening night. Now, 25 years later, these memories come flooding back as I sit beside my brother, watching him

1

swiftly dart through congested traffic while responding to an armed robbery call. You see, although I hung up my "six-shooter" years ago, he didn't. As a Metro Nashville Police Officer, he now holsters a 9mm semiautomatic in place of the cap gun.

And suddenly, the game of "cops and robbers" is for real.

This book was written with the intent of providing a glimpse of what life behind the badge is really like. Some of the stories you may find humorous. Others might leave you wondering just how low humanity has sunk in our society. Either way, they should dispel the myth that the main thrust of policework is straddling the counter at Dunkin' Donuts and meeting ticket quotas.

Although various suspect's names, dates, descriptions and locations of certain events may have been altered in order to protect the privacy of those individuals involved, the essence of the stories themselves are true. And for each story brought to life in the following pages, there are hundreds more like them from the thousands of officers donning their "blues" everywhere.

I hope the underlying theme in this book will quickly become self-evident...that beneath the badge and gun, cops are human beings, just like everyone else. They laugh; they cry. They have their good days, as well as those where they would just as soon chunk the shield and find a job scrapping barnacles off rusty freighters for a living. Like people everywhere, they worry about their kids growing up, the mortgage payments on their houses, and providing a safe and secure environment for their families. But in addition to their own concerns, they must also confront and respond to the problems of a tumultuous society each and every day.

That combination can be a heavy load to bear.

Case in point: On Christmas Day, 1994, Officer Timothy Torres finished his morning sandwich at a Times Square restaurant in New York. Instead of going back out on patrol, however, he quietly sat in a booth, put his .38 caliber service-revolver to his head, and pulled the trigger while fellow officers watched in horror. Underscoring this tragedy is the fact that Torres was the 12th officer in New York City to commit suicide in 1994.

Earlier that morning, his final task as a police officer was persuading an emotionally disturbed man to go to the hospital. Like many other cops, Torres was so consumed in the challenge of helping others, he didn't find the time or means to seek help himself.

I'd like to thank the officers of the Metro Nashville Police Department-East Station, for their hospitality and friendship during my research for this book. Considering that until recently, they endured several years without any meaningful pay increase, these people deserve more recognition than can be given here for being motivated enough to continuously put themselves on the line for the rest of us on a daily basis.

A special thanks goes to my wife, Brenda, for patiently allowing me to absorb myself in this project and for guiding me towards the right words to express certain thoughts after my creative well had run dry. Thanks also to Dough Hubler, a talented writer, artist and close friend, for letting his wit and wisdom rub off on me. My appreciation also goes to "Captain" Bob Beals...looks like some of our thoughts on another book wound up in this one. Last, but certainly not least, I'd like to extend a special tribute to professor emeritus Jack Higgs from East Tennessee State University for his immaculate editing of this book. His advice and contacts helped make this publication a reality. Known as both a renowned English professor and writer, he has published such books as

"Appalachia Inside Out" and "God In The Stadium: Sports And Religion In America".

Turning the attention now to those who are ever anxious to assume the role of judge and jury while scrutinizing a cop's every move, I pass along the appropriate words of Teddy Roosevelt in tribute to those who have experienced both the tragedy and triumph of wearing a badge:

"It is not the critic who counts, not the man who points out how the strong man stumbles or where the doer of deeds could have done them better. The credit belongs to the man *who is actually in the arena,* whose face is marred by dust and sweat and blood, who strives valiantly, who errs and comes up short again and again because there is no effort without error and shortcomings, who knows the great devotion, who spends himself in a worthy cause, who at the best knows in the end the high achievement of triumph and who at worst, if he fails while daring greatly, knows his place shall never be with those timid and cold souls who know neither victory nor defeat."

And now, welcome to life on the other side.

PRELUDE

It happened early on a cool fall morning, as the stars still reflected brightly during the waning moments of darkness. Alarm clocks throughout the city were poised to impatiently summon the sleeping with their intrusive beckoning; the welcome aroma of coffee filtering through the air would soon follow. Night was slowly turning into day, another day in which people would wake and continue their normal lives filled with abundant hopes and dreams, of endless tomorrows. For one man, however, these visions of the future abruptly ended without a moment's notice.

At 4:55 a.m., October 10, 1991, a barrage of shots echoed down a side-street in Nashville, and a soldier fell...mortally wounded.

When the news of his death flashed across the television screens, people in the city paused, reflecting their sorrow with transparent interest, then continued on without missing a step. After all, he was just a cop. He was just doing his job. It's risky, but hell, *that's what we pay them to do.*

It was just another man, just another name...

Lt. James Ronnie Woodard may have sensed that death would be his companion the morning of October 10th. Several hours earlier, he had eerily recounted to some friends how dangerous police work was.

"He had a feeling that he wouldn't be here tonight...he suspected that he'd die soon," said a relative to the owner of a motel where Woodard moonlighted as a security guard in an effort to make ends meet on a police officer's salary.

A little less than two hours after making this statement, Woodard's body lay upon the barren asphalt, life rapidly ebbing from him as his blood seeped across the pavement of a darkened parking lot. Moments earlier, a suspect in a car theft had fired five shots point blank at Woodard, riddling his torso and sending him plummeting to the ground. Miraculously, Woodard somehow managed to fire a lone shot in defense, wounding the suspect in the buttocks.

It was a courageous act fueled by instinct and desperation, but it was too little, too late.

Portions of the following transcript of radio conversations between central dispatch, Lt. Woodard, the trucker who found him, and the officers looking for him appeared shortly afterwards in the *Nashville Banner*. As the transmission begins at 4:51 a.m., Woodard - identified as unit 705 - asks the dispatcher for a check on license number DVH055.

Dispatcher: 10-4, David, Victor, Henry 055, 1988 Honda Prelude to a David Duncan at 413 Rockwood Drive in Hermitage. And 705, it's going to be a 10-72 (stolen) vehicle.

Woodard: OK, I've got it.

Dispatcher: What's your location?

Woodard: It won't stop...

Dispatcher: 705, what's your location?

Long pause

Woodard: Shot! (garbled)

Dispatcher: 705, try it again.

Unidentified officer: He's been working next to John right out...(unintelligible) on Murfreesboro Road.

Dispatcher: Headquarters to any car that may be close to 411 Murfreesboro.

Pause

Car 23: Tom, he's not at 411. I'll check around some more.

Pause

Mike Hayes (trucker): Please, hey, have you got a copy? I'm here at this police car! He's been hurt, right here,

6

let's see, at the corner of Fesslers Lane and Enis Reed at this Dominion Bank! Please, have you got a copy?

Dispatcher: 10-4, are you advising the officer's hurt?

Hayes: Yes, ma'am, I just passed by and seen somebody. I don't know if he's shot or what. But he's down on the ground, and I'm in the truck right here! Please hurry! He's got a gun in his hand...please hurry, I'm out here at the Dominion Bank!

The suspect, Timothy Ford, was later arrested and charged with murder. Out on parole, Ford had apparently broken into a house and stolen several personal items along with the car, and was heading across town when stopped by Woodard. Having been arrested 15 times over the previous nine years, Ford knew what he would be facing if he let Woodard take him into custody. What went through Ford's mind at that point can only be assumed. But somehow, through his own twisted logic, he came to the conclusion it was better to take the life of a police officer than to lose his freedom once again.

As an 18-year veteran of the force, Woodard was known as a cop who never stopped policing, someone who aggressively enforced the law. But there was more than this generic, one-dimensional side to Woodard. He was also regarded as a man who cared for people. His friends will always remember the day in 1974 when he dangled over the Shelby Avenue bridge for 10 minutes, risking his life while clinging onto the arm of a man considering suicide before finally being able to pull him to safety.

And now, Lt. Ronnie Woodard will be known for something he never intended. He was the 232nd police officer to die in the line of duty in Tennessee.

Whenever a fellow officer is slain, a piece of our own soul vanishes with them as well. And after 14 years on the force, sometimes mine feels like Swiss cheese.

Perhaps it's true. Only the good die young.

Metro Police Sgt. Gary Young sits on the steps of Dominion Bank, Fessler's Lane Branch, after his friend and fellow officer Lt. James Ronnie Woodard was shot in the bank's parking lot. Young was Woodard's partner during Woodard's rookie year in 1973. (photo courtesy Freeman Ramsey, *THE TENNESSEAN*)

1

GENESIS

Perhaps two of the most frequently asked questions a police officer hears from those outside our profession are: *Why did you become a cop,* and *what's it like?*

A quick response isn't easy. Summarizing Tolstoy's *War and Peace,* or even the Bible in 200 words or less would be an easier task.

No one is born with the desire to enter the field of law enforcement any more than they are conceived with the inherent urge to become a doctor, a politician or even a brick mason. Instead, it would seem the desire to enter any occupation is related to the various events we experience in the socialization process from youth to adulthood that guides us in a certain direction. Though Freud may have reason to argue this theory, it seems reasonable to stick by it since he's currently unable to debate the matter.

When people choose a career as a police officer, they willfully step over the line into another world, an arena where certain harsh realities are exposed...the same realities most elect to ignore or pretend don't exist. Time after time, many of the circumstances confronting officers are some of the worst and most livid life has to offer. It's hard to overemphasize this point, because unless you *actually experience these events,* they are many times reduced to 2 x 3 column inches in a local newspaper, quickly read and just as quickly forgotten. However, in the life of a cop, these stories take on a reality of their own.

Throughout my years with the Metropolitan Nashville Police Department, I've seen people victimized by brutal crimes for no sane reason, people whose lives have been literally ripped apart and forever changed as a result of some senseless action committed by individuals who couldn't give a damn about anyone but themselves. I've sadly seen innocent children abused from unforgivable molestation, and I have viewed too many of their mangled bodies after a drunken driver had taken their precious lives. I've even watched in disbelief as prostitutes, eight to nine months pregnant, continue to turn tricks in order to support their drug habit.

I've lived other people's nightmares, such as having the unforgettable stench of burnt human flesh pierce my nostrils while pulling someone's charred remains out of a fiery auto accident to confronting the tragedy of seeing peoples' lives slowly drain away after they had shot themselves in the head, apparently convinced death would be less painful than life. I've also felt the remorse, the bitter frustration over the loss of fellow officers who bravely lived and died wearing the thin metal shield that many look at with disdain and venomously spit upon with contempt.

And throughout many events, I've encountered the innocent people who suffered at the hands of others, while some of the guilty slide through the judicial system with nothing more than a proverbial slap on the wrist. Justice is often a matter of opinion, a concept with varying degrees, and in a litigious society such as ours, sometimes it's difficult to determine where the law ends...and justice begins.

And still people ask me, *why did you become a cop,* and *what's it like?*

Coming up with a definitive answer is not easy. How do you describe a profession to someone who simply cannot comprehend the emotions behind the events we have to continuously deal with? Can you remember the last time you tried to explain to a hysterical woman that she couldn't enter her father's apartment because it was a crime scene, and he was beaten to death over mere pocket change? Have you ever confronted PCP-crazed teenagers, foaming at the mouth as they held a gun to their head while screaming they were possessed by the devil and must sacrifice themselves for the world to be saved?

Stephen King and Alfred Hitchcock, please step aside. We're dealing with reality here, and it rides up front.

Life behind the badge isn't so neatly-scripted as portrayed on *Dragnet*, and it's definitely not as action-packed as the *Dirty Harry* movies. No offense, Clint; the movies are a great box-office draw, but not many cities can afford the insurance premiums to cover your methods of crime control.

Slice and dice it anyway you want, but it all shakes out to long periods of routine followed by short bursts of insanity. Policework can be as boring as unbuttered toast or as crazy as an insane asylum.

If a comparison had to be drawn, the television series *Hill Street Blues*, even with its limitations, would come closest to being fairly representative. This show's underlying theme conveyed a simple and unrelenting truth. When individuals decide to pin a badge on their chest, they expose themselves to a complicated way of life that is constantly thrown off center with new and complex human variables.

Being a cop isn't just something you do; it's something that you are. It goes far beyond simply performing a routine and collecting a paycheck. It becomes a lifestyle, and to some, a sense of purpose.

Although it's difficult to pinpoint the reasons why a person chooses to become a police officer, the reasons not to are more obvious: The long hours, varied shift work, disparagingly low pay, the disrespect and discouragement of wearing a badge, the risk of being injured attempting to help those with an attitude of indifference, or working within an inequitable legal system which can leave you pounding your head against a brick wall in frustration at day's end.

In addition to the above-mentioned "fringe benefits," the courts have ruled that a police officer can be sued personally as well as departmentally. As such, not only can cops lose their job in a lawsuit, but everything else as well.

Given these reasons, it's understandable why someone would question *how anyone could rationalize the thought of becoming a police officer.*

There is, however, a flip side to this occupation. Or, as Paul Harvey might say, "the rest of the story."

Being a cop may entail certain pitfalls, but there are numerous intangible rewards which come along with this profession as well. It's the opportunity to live on the cutting edge, to take on the constant challenges life on the street offers. It's being the only one the sick and injured can depend upon until medical help arrives. It's assisting in the miracle of birth, and holding the newborn child in your arms that you helped bring into this world unexpectedly. It's giving people a fighting chance against anarchy, and feeling the satisfaction of putting those who wreak havoc on our society behind bars before they can spread their destruction even further.

Or, as one officer not-so-eloquently summed up, "it's stackin', rackin' and packin' dirtbags in an 8 x 10 cell."

Simply put, it's the chance to make the kind of contribution to society that few jobs offer; it provides you with a sense of pride, a source of self-respect and fulfillment in knowing that you *can make a meaningful difference in the lives of others.*

Reasons aside, one fact stands clear. As police officers, we are united in the purpose to serve and protect society, to uphold the laws the public has deemed necessary to enact through their chosen representation in governmental offices.

13

Though this purpose may sound somewhat simplistic, the implementation of these responsibilities is far more difficult.

And that, as they say, is where the story begins.

*   *   *   *   *   *

The "itch" began in 1978, when I was 23. Before long, it developed into a full-blown rash.

Although I didn't realize it in the beginning, my career path to becoming a police officer (sometimes pronounced *poe-lease* by those with a heavy southern drawl, as if they were speaking through a mouthful of grandma's mashed 'taters') began amidst the shouts of *"it's Friday night, we're three waitresses short, so who's gonna handle tables four through seven?* and *"the intercom system to the curb has crashed, cars are packing the lot, what do you want us to do?"*

As store manager for a Shoney's Restaurant in Madison, Tennessee, I had the opportunity, during quieter times, to meet with the various officers who provided security for the occasionally rambunctious drive-in section of the restaurant. Weekends transformed this area into a cruising haven for local teenagers, who engaged in the pre-mating ritual of circling the stalls for hours, vying for the attention of the opposite sex as they throttled the massive V-8's rumbling beneath freshly-waxed metal skins.

One of the officers stationed there was Charles "Buck" Buchannan, who is now a sergeant on my detail. While becoming friends with "Buck", I found myself looking forward to our frequent curbside chats about his job. All the stories surrounding his career were intriguing; I couldn't listen to enough of them. I was like a kid hooked on Nintendo.

Another officer, Ed Stanfield, lived in the same apartment complex that I did. Ed and I became good friends, and sensing my interest in police work, he invited me to ride with him during his shift several times. During these eight-hour sprees, a whole new side of life unfolded before me. As I began to *experience* the situations I had listened to with curiosity before, I knew the seed of change was being planted. The hours I spent on patrol with Ed added extra fuel to my growing ambitions, and it wasn't long afterwards that I decided to bid farewell to the food-service industry and devote my energies to pursuing a career in law enforcement.

The first order of business was obtaining an application and fingerprint card from the city's department of personnel. Upon completing these, I turned them over to the police department, and several months later was notified that I would be starting the test sequence.

The initial stage in the testing process was the physical agility course, which consisted of several grueling and intense phases. As fate would have it, the kitchen manager of the Shoney's I worked at showed up the same afternoon to take the agility test as well. After getting over the awkward surprise of seeing each other, we agreed to keep our off-hours activities between ourselves. Realizing we were risking our current jobs for a shot at becoming police officers, neither of us wanted to be standing side by side in the unemployment line if word got back to those who signed our paychecks.

The next segment of the testing program was the civil-service exam, which was a combination intelligence and aptitude test. Many of the applicants who performed well on the agility course found themselves weeded out at this point. The kitchen manager, unfortunately, was one of these casualties.

The polygraph test followed and proved to be an experience unto itself. During this "mental enema," no subject was taboo. Discussing such items as work history, driving record and personal finances was easy enough, but when the questions turned to topics such as deviant sexual practices, I started to feel like I was being interviewed by Howard Stern.

Wrapping up the session, the examiner asked one final question. "Mr. Fielden, what political magazines do you subscribe to?"

"Right now, TIME magazine is the only one I receive."

The examiner didn't say anything but continued to stare in my direction.

"Would that...be considered political?" I asked, hoping to find out where his question was leading.

"It would if you belonged to the *WEATHERMEN*."

Being naive, I silently wondered what the weather had to do with anything. It wasn't until several days later I learned that the *WEATHERMEN* was a political group I'd never heard of.

After submitting to a medical examination, a psychological profile analysis and an interview with a psychiatrist, I was nearing the end of the lengthy testing process. Or, I should say, at least the police department testing.

My resolve was being tested at home in a different manner. It was during this time my first wife and I were experiencing some marital problems. My quest to join the police department wasn't helping matters any, and one evening when this discussion came up, she issued the ultimatum. If I became a cop, she would find her comfort elsewhere. Her reasoning was she wanted her husband to have a "normal" job, where he would be safely home at nights and off weekends. I reluctantly gave into her wishes, and sent the personnel department a letter stating I would be withdrawing my application.

I later discovered this wasn't the only source of conflict we had. Unable to reconcile our differences, we split up for the final time, and I immediately resubmitted my application. Fortunately, the only test I had to repeat was the physical agility course, which once again left me with aching muscles for an entire week.

I would have plenty of time to recover, however, for the country was in a mild recession at the time. This forced the department to mandate a hiring freeze on police officers for almost two years. The testing process wasn't rushed during this period; in fact, several months often lapsed between tests. Getting used to the idea of not knowing if or when I would get the opportunity to become a police officer was something I reluctantly learned to tolerate.

My anticipation eased somewhat the day I received a letter from the department stating that I had been scheduled for an interview with the Chief of Police, who at the time was Joe Casey. The final hurdle to clear was in sight at last.

I vividly recall walking into Chief Casey's office on the morning of my appointment. Confronting me were five distinguished looking men wearing crisply-pressed uniforms. They had enough brass and ribbons on their chests to open a gift shop. For an eternity of two minutes, they quietly studied the folders spread out on the table in front of them. Trying to remain calm, I found myself shifting uncomfortably on my heels as I awaited the questioning to begin. Chief Casey was the first to speak.

"Mr. Fielden, do you feel police officers have the right to strike?"

"No sir," I quickly responded. When the Police Chief asks a question, you don't waste his time by making him wait for an answer. "It would affect public safety if a strike took place."

He gazed at my folder for a long moment. "I see that you applied once before. What happened?"

"Well, sir," I began, carefully choosing my words, "to make a long story short, my former wife threatened to leave me if I joined the department. I've remarried since then, so I shouldn't have that same problem."

The thick air of tension melted away as laughter filled the room, prompting a sigh of relief from my chest. Perhaps now, I thought, I was a bit closer to being accepted into the training academy.

Several weeks later, I came home from work one afternoon and picked up a message on the answering machine instructing me to call Sergeant Hunley at the training academy. Stomach in knots, I immediately dialed his number. When he came to the phone, I was the recipient of a short, to the point conversation. "Go to R and R Uniforms on 8th Avenue South tomorrow to be measured. Report to the training academy Monday morning at 8:00, wearing a suit and tie, a short haircut, and bring with you a 2000 word essay about yourself. Oh, and I hope you've been doing some running..."

On Monday, October 16, 1980, I embarked on the adventure...

2

THE INITIATION

The ominous theme to *Jaws* floated through my mind like a Gregorian chant the first morning I arrived at the training academy. For the next 14 weeks, I would be subjected to a comprehensive "high-stress" training regimen, one that would physically and mentally challenge my limits to the extreme. Unlike military training, however, cadets are allowed, even encouraged, to leave if the program gets too tough for them to handle.

The reason training is geared to be difficult should be as obvious as the price tag dangling from Minnie Pearl's hat. Life on the streets is tough. By learning how to cope with the stress in training, you become better prepared for the real-life confrontations that only a Mike Tyson would welcome.

The first day at the academy started out in the finest of boot camp traditions. After registration, our class was escorted out into the courtyard where we were instructed on formation procedures, how to walk in military fashion and the accepted protocol of standing at attention. After getting acquainted with these basic disciplines, we regrouped in a classroom to view several "officer survival films." Once the projector started running, it became clear that we weren't watching some Disney classic from the Family Channel. These movies depicted officers performing routine events, such as making traffic stops and knocking on suspect's doors. In the next instant, someone would blow these unfortunate officers away in graphic detail. As we sat in our seats, transfixed at the events unfolding on the screen, a sergeant came into the classroom and proceeded to recount all the negative aspects of becoming a cop. This included handing out a sheet of paper detailing the local officers who were assaulted the previous year, categorized by those shot, cut, bitten, hit by cars, etc. As I recall, the list was rather long.

I imagine this was done in order to eliminate those who had any doubts as to what they were getting into. It worked, and our class had a few empty seats the following day.

The second morning, the remainder of the class met in the gym and received khaki-colored uniforms with officer trainee patches sewn onto them. We were now officially "plebes," a term used to describe underclassmen in the military. After suiting up, the majority of us were told that our freshly-cropped hair was too long to pass inspection. That night I went back to the barber, only to have to return again the following day after being informed my hair was still "too long" (long being defined as over 1 1/2 inches). When I finally passed inspection, my hair was so short it wouldn't lay down on the sides. Instead, it spiked sideways and resembled a five o'clock shadow. I took what little comfort I could in knowing that my head wouldn't be the only one getting cold in our class.

The physical training ("P.T.-Good For You, Good For Me," as it was known at the academy) was rigorous. After fine-tuning our formation marching skills, we progressed to the point of running five miles a day, rain or shine. Added to this was the "daily dozen", twelve different calisthenics involving high repetitions that would've made Arnold Schwarzenegger fight for his breath. Since the physical training was considered as important as the classroom studies, we were periodically tested on the agility course and timed runs. Our class lost two trainees the day before graduation after they were unable to complete the two-mile run under the required time.

The classroom instruction taxed us mentally just as the workouts did physically. We were lectured and tested in the areas of law, psychological stress management, sociology, criminology, defensive driving, force utilization, patrol tactics, emergency medical care, report writing, human relations, accident investigations, radio/computer operations and officer survival methods. During the 14 weeks at the academy, we received more hours of criminal law instruction than law schools provide.

Tests were numerous. A general test was given each week and minor exams every other day. If a cadet failed two general tests, or any of the law, firearms or emergency medical training exams, they were immediately dismissed from the academy.

The firearms portion of the training consisted of two entire weeks on the firing range. Rumor has it that one reason for such extensive instruction is to ensure that when an officer arrives at a burglary-in-progress call and a suspect runs out shooting, the officer is able to hit the suspect when returning fire, not the little old lady two blocks down the street who picked a bad time to go out and check her mailbox.

The firearms training also included the traditional "good-guy, bad-guy" course, where the cadet encounters different targets which spontaneously appear at various locations. On some of the targets were pictures of elderly people brandishing weapons, empty-handed thugs and children waving water pistols. Response time is crucial, since the cadets don't have the luxury to think consciously; they must instead react as their training and instinct have taught them. The ramifications of making the wrong decision in actual instances like these on the street are obvious.

Of particular interest was the night-firing training taught at the state prison. Here, shrouded in darkness, we would practice shooting with only the muzzle flash to aim our weapons. Following this, low-level lights were turned on, which signaled trainee teams to jump into a cruiser, flip on the siren and emergency lights, drive to the end of a road, then bail out and start firing at a target. Besides the difficulty of adjusting to shooting in this type of situation, many of us had to contend with the fact that we had never *actually driven* a police car before. When adrenaline is furiously pumping throughout your body and you leap into an unfamiliar vehicle crammed full of strange instrumentation and electronic equipment, finding the ignition switch ain't easy.

Sandwiched between our many other assignments were the defensive tactics classes. Ken Pence, an officer and a black belt, provided the instruction and spoke the first and final words when it came to the art of hand-to-hand combat. Everyone dreaded getting called into the ring at *Ken's House of Pain* in order for him to demonstrate fighting techniques because the result was...well, usually painful. Still, the hours we spent fighting, handcuffing and learning the proper search and weapon retention methods under Ken's watchful eyes would prove invaluable.

Seasoned officers arrived at the academy when it was time to learn the procedures involved in felony car stops. Having already earned their "street degrees" many times over, they knew every imaginable way to confuse a trainee since they had encountered their fair share of unusual circumstances in the field. It was interesting to watch how cadets responded when these officers refused to get out of a car when ordered to, or would step out from the vehicle speaking Spanish, or perhaps emerge pointing to their ears as if they were hard of hearing in spite of repeated commands by the cadet. Of course, the novelty of it all quickly wore off when it was *your* turn in the limelight.

The hectic pace of the training schedule continued until the day that once seemed unreachable finally arrived. On

22

February 2, 1981, graduation ceremonies were held for the 41 of us who had the dedication and endurance to follow through with the ambitions we had unpacked 14 weeks earlier. Our class originally had close to 65 trainees.

To this day, I fondly recall dressing in full uniform for the first time in preparation for the formal graduation ceremonies. A flood of adrenaline rushed through my body as I stood facing a mirror, viewing the reflection of the person I had become. The pride, the sense of satisfaction over my accomplishments to obtain the right to wear "the blues" was etched into the smile which slowly grew across my face.

Despite the malice and indignation I would soon receive from some in recognition of the authority that the uniform represents, I was nonetheless proud to be wearing it. The transformation had occurred. For better or worse, I was now a police officer.

And the *real education* was about to begin.

Officer Mark Fielden

3

LAWN DARTS AND OTHER LETHAL WEAPONS

Nashville, Tennessee is situated in Davidson County, which is nestled along the majestic Cumberland River in Middle Tennessee, and encompasses approximately 533 square miles.

At one time, Davidson County was like any other large county, and had both a sheriff's department and a city police department, city and county schools, separate governing bodies and all the duplication of services that goes along with this type of system.

In the 1960's, the voters of Davidson County decided to change the governmental structure. Davidson County and Nashville were thus consolidated into one entity, ruled by one governing body. As of the 1980 census, approximately 500,000 people inhabited this area.

Nashville, affectionately nicknamed the "Music City", is home to numerous major recording studios and the prominent tv/recording stars that patronize them. Barbara Mandrell, Randy Travis, Garth Brooks, Steve Winwood, Mel Tillis and Charlie Daniels are just a few of the successful entertainers living in this area. The rising young stars of tomorrow are in abundance here as well, and for a buck-fifty cover charge and a two-drink minimum, you can enjoy these struggling unknown talents in any number of local taverns as they try to make a name for themselves in the recording business.

In addition to being the state's capitol, Nashville is also the home of numerous tourist attractions, such as The Grand Old Opry and the Opryland amusement park. Vanderbilt University is also located here, as well as the Vanderbilt Medical Center, which has a reputation of being one of the premier cancer research and treatment centers in the nation.

On the industrial front, Nashville's location, mild climate and scenic beauty complement the population's strong Southern work ethic in order to entice numerous national companies to locate their corporate headquarters within the area.

Like any bustling metropolis, however, there is another side of Nashville that is not so neatly gift-wrapped. We have our share of homicides, rapes, prostitution, robberies, domestic violence and drug problems any city of this size experiences.

Out of all the challenges police officers face, domestic disputes are generally the ones we dislike the most. Unlike a number of other calls we respond to, there is usually no "tidy" ending to these situations. Normally, the best officers can hope for on a domestic is to calm everyone down for the time being, and hope we don't receive another call to return a few minutes after leaving. Even when we have to arrest one of the parties, it's usually only a temporary solution, as it's not uncommon to receive additional calls to the same address soon after the subject is released from jail. After awhile, you begin to feel like all you're doing is postponing the inevitable meltdown of a relationship.

The inherent danger of responding to a domestic situation mirrors human nature. A person's behavior can quickly become irrational and unpredictable when strong emotions are involved. To make matters worse, the responding officer is often viewed as an outsider who has violated the privacy of one's home, an unwelcome arbitrator interfering with personal matters. As a result, the individuals may unify their hostilities

26

and turn on you like fanatical fans at a Colombian soccer match while you're trying to referee the situation.

The bottom line is that it really doesn't matter if someone lives in the projects or an upscale suburban mansion; during a heated domestic argument, the same naked aggression is present... regardless of social class.

Too often, there is just no winning in these situations, and a temporary "cease-fire" is the best that can be negotiated. To further highlight the magnitude of this problem, statistics show that in 1990 over 22,000 Tennessee women and children fled to safe-house shelters to escape domestic abuse. A surprisingly high figure? Not when you consider that nationwide, a woman is battered by a spouse or boyfriend every 15 seconds, 90% of the time in front of the frightened eyes of young children. In all, an estimated 4 million children witness the horrors of domestic violence each year. These alarming figures were recently revealed on Dateline NBC during an interview between co-host Stone Phillips and Sgt. Mark Wynn of the Metro Nashville Police Department. In addition to his other duties, Sgt. Wynn specializes in teaching fellow officers how to handle domestic disputes, and has received national recognition for his efforts in helping those caught in the web of domestic violence. His expertise in this field wasn't merely acquired through research, however. The foundation of his knowledge was built by growing up in the living hell of it.

As small children, both Mark and his brother watched helplessly as their mother was continuously beaten by their alcoholic stepfather during his drunken rampages. Finally, there came a day they could no longer stand to watch the abuse. Since they weren't big enough to physically challenge the man, another way to stop him would have to be found. A plan was soon born.

While their stepfather slept one afternoon, Mark and his brother sneaked into his bedroom and spiked the wine bottle on his nightstand with RAID. Confident they had just solved the cycle of abuse, they quietly went into the living room and patiently waited for him to wake up and finish off the bottle, anticipating he would "croak like a roach." Although only children, Mark and his brother had seen their stepfather's drunken assaults long enough to have no reservations about their actions.

Some children turn out to be abusers themselves after growing up in an environment wrecked by domestic violence. Others, like Mark Wynn, become driven with the ambition to make a positive impact in the lives of others who face the situations he did as a child.

And his stepfather? It turned out that he suffered no ill effects from the RAID put into his wine. As a matter of fact, he drank the rest of the bottle, unaware of the special ingredient added. He lived for several years after the incident and continued his drinking and abusive routines.

As fate would have it, the first call I answered when on patrol by myself was a domestic call. This was just after I had completed the customary six month probationary period and was no longer under the protective wing of a senior officer.

"Unit 12, responding to the 10-41 (domestic disturbance) at 201 Windridge Colony Drive," I replied with an air of confidence to the dispatcher. After months of training and preparation, I had finally been assigned my own cruiser and a specific zone to patrol. It was, I thought, my own corner of the world to oversee, an area in which I was determined to make an impact.

I was pumped and ready. I was going to make a difference in the lives of those I encountered, even if it was only my first day solo.

Right.

I pulled into the complainant's address and was met at the sidewalk by a man yelling that his son was threatening to harm his wife with a knife. His wife and son stood several yards behind him and returned my stare in silence. About halfway through the man's explanation of what had happened, it suddenly dawned on me that these people were looking to me, *and only me*, for the solution to their problems. I then began to realize just how unprepared I was to deal with the complexity of domestic situations. Fortunately, an officer with more experience than I happened to drive by at the time, and together we were able to work out a temporary solution.

Part of the solution, I humbly reminded myself while trying to patch up my confidence, was I still had a lot to learn.

The most frustrating part of dealing with some domestic calls (especially those where physical violence is present) is the unwillingness of the victims to follow through with prosecution once their case comes up in court. The typical scenario involves officers responding to a domestic call from a victim, generally a female, who is often hysterical when officers arrive. Angry as a disturbed nest of hornets, she wants the police to arrest the husband or boyfriend. By the time the case is heard in court, the man involved has convinced the victim that he's sorry, he'll never harm her again, and in the future "it will be different." Either by intimidation or a smooth job of salesmanship, he convinces her to drop the charges as they stand before the judge, hand in hand.

This infuriates both judges and police officers, because of the inability to remedy the problem and for the wasted time and effort put in to obtain prosecution.

A classic example of this type of situation occurred several years ago on a domestic call Officer Charles Harrison and I were drawn into.

It was on a weekend, about 4 a.m., when a 10-41 was called in from a trailer park on Dickerson Road. Since Charles was the closest unit in the vicinity, he fielded the call and made his way to the reported location.

When he pulled up to the address, a young lady emerged from a small travel trailer. Her T-shirt and blue jean shorts were smeared with grass stains and dirt. Storming to his cruiser, she screamed that her newlywed husband had tried to run over her with their car. She pointed to an assortment of scrapes and bruises on her legs as she shook with anger, explaining they were the result of rolling on the ground to keep from getting hit. This, along with the circular marks in the gravel in front of the trailer, was enough to give her story credibility.

Although her husband sped off moments before Charles arrived, she was determined to make him pay for his actions. Infuriated, she demanded that the police do something, and threatened to complain to the mayor if she didn't receive any cooperation.

As you might have guessed, trying to run over someone with a car is a felony. In order to assist the victim, Charles went to night court and obtained a vehicular assault warrant on her husband. Not long afterwards, he made another sweep of the trailer park and radioed me that the suspect's car was back in the driveway.

I quickly arrived at the address to provide Charles backup. It was still dark outside, which allowed us to pull into the trailer park without being seen. From a short distance we could see a dim light casting a hazy shadow within the rear of the trailer, but there didn't appear to be any movement inside.

Knowing the trailer had only one entrance, Charles and I cautiously made our way to the front door. We listened for a moment before knocking, trying to get an idea of what we were about to confront.

The wind was sweeping throughout the fallen autumn leaves covering the ground around us, creating a soft whisper as it spiraled downward into the shallow chasms beneath the trailer. From the depth of these sounds, a muffled moan seemed to rise, then quickly drifted away as the wind subsided.

A sudden flicker of the light in the back window took my attention from the strange sound. The dim glow we'd seen from the drive began to shimmer. *The room was lit by a candle*, I realized. Thoughts of ritualistic killings rushed through my mind. Given the violent nature of her husband, we had to assume he was capable of anything. If he knew she had called the police in order to have him arrested, her safety may have been further jeopardized.

Then I heard it again. A low, moaning sound, the kind of sound a wounded animal might make. This time I knew it wasn't the wind, but was coming from inside the trailer. Charles immediately cocked his head towards the door, confirming that it wasn't my imagination.

"She may be hurt. We've gotta move," I whispered.

"Police! Open the door!" Charles yelled, banging on the metal door as hard as he could. The pane glass windows throughout the trailer vibrated in unison from the force of his pounding.

Without warning, the door suddenly jerked opened and from the shadows emerged the young lady who had demanded our help. She stood in the doorway for a long moment, her face red with a mixture of anger and embarrassment, trying to catch her breath. Wrapped loosely around her small figure was a revealing pink bathrobe which left little to the imagination.

"What do you want?" she screamed, staring coldly at us.

Charles and I exchanged puzzled looks. We were both taken by surprise with her change of behavior. Two hours ago, she demanded that her husband be arrested. Now, clearly not too happy to see us, she wanted to know what we wanted.

"Ma'am, we have the warrant for your husband's arrest," Charles responded.

"I don't want him arrested! Now get out of here!" she shot back.

"Ma'am, this arrest warrant, *that you requested we obtain*, is an official order to take your husband in front of a judge," I interrupted. "We can't leave without him. It will be up to you and the judge to decide if you want to prosecute."

She momentarily met my reply with an icy stare, then glanced over her petite shoulder towards the back bedroom. As she turned her head, Charles and I tried to step into the trailer. Sensing our movement, she sprung with the prowess of a linebacker to block our entry.

"I said get outta here, you're not needed and sure the hell not wanted, dammit!"

"Look, if you don't let us do our job, we'll have to arrest you for interfering with a police officer," I said, trying to control the frustration in my voice.

As I reached out to move her aside, she quickly jerked away, causing her robe to fall open and reveal a tiny pair of white bikini panties, complete with a big red heart on the front. Apparently, she and her husband had been in the process of "making-up" when we arrived. However, by law, we still had a warrant to serve.

"Damn you both, you're messing everything up!" she cried, clinching her fists in anger. As she took a wild swing in our direction, I stepped back just in time to keep my nose intact.

"Enough!" Charles yelled. *"Now you're under arrest!"*

Hearing this, she collapsed into a corner, wrapping her arms tightly against herself and continued to scream at us with all the might she could muster.

"This is getting ridiculous. I'm gonna call for a female officer," Charles snorted.

Not a bad idea, I thought, since the lady was still half-naked and refused to budge from the kitchen floor.

Soon after another unit arrived and took the couple into custody, I left the scene and checked back into service. As I drove off into a brilliant early-morning sunrise, I couldn't help but wonder the odds of the newlyweds celebrating their first anniversary together.

Only Jimmy the Greek would know for sure. Unfortunately, however, I didn't have his phone number.

Just as the attitudes, beliefs and values of society evolve over time, so does the law. In a never-ending process, outdated laws are discarded and newer ones, those reflecting a more enlightened culture, are added.

Prior to the new domestic law established in 1990, domestic calls were handled very differently. Many years ago, when officers discovered a call was domestic in nature, they would abruptly leave, telling those involved to work out whatever problems on their own. Even if the complainant had a bruised nose and bloody lip, there wasn't much we could legally do, since simple assault is a misdemeanor, and an officer must personally witness a misdemeanor take place in order to make an arrest (unless the victim or a witness voluntarily signs a warrant).

In these cases, the police were powerless to act unless the victim wanted us to intercede. Unfortunately, because they were usually afraid of creating an even bigger problem, they would seldom prosecute. Many times, the victim would just want us to make the abuser "stop hitting them," without having to place the family member or acquaintance under arrest. That's a tough balancing act to pull off.

As a result, professionals in the domestic violence field convinced the state lawmakers that a new domestic violence law was needed. In response, the Tennessee State Legislature declared that officers may make arrests on assaults if they have probable cause an assault did happen and that more violence would likely occur if an arrest is not made. This gave us the power to initiate arrests on domestic assault cases, even if the victim was afraid to do so.

Although this was a positive step towards addressing domestic violence, it did contain a drawback. Officer discretion was severely curtailed.

Remember, the law states an officer **may** make an arrest - it doesn't say they **have** to. This same concept is applied to DUI enforcement. The officer is free to make an arrest, but they aren't forced to. However, should we let a drunk driver go, and the intoxicated soul continues down the street and kills someone in an accident, guess who's going to be liable in a civil suit for contributory negligence? Your friendly neighborhood cop, of course.

The bottom line is that if you leave the scene of a domestic disturbance where someone was hurt, and you didn't make an arrest (assuming the suspect is still there), you'd better be quick in putting all your assets into a buddy's name.

Nowadays, if we respond to a domestic call involving an injured individual, someone is probably going to jail. We have the duty to protect the victim, to initiate an arrest, and because we must protect ourselves against civil suits, we're likely to exercise our legal options.

Although arrests have increased since the new domestic law went into effect, there have been fewer repeated calls to the same addresses. Also, should a spouse be assaulted for a third time, the charge of aggravated assault (a felony) can be filed, with harsher consequences resulting.

It's time someone put their foot down on domestic abuse, and that foot belongs to us.

There's an old proverb which goes *"he who waves a fist at his wife during breakfast may wind up sipping soup through a straw at dinner."* Poetic justice, so to speak.

James and Jolene Hunt, united in blissless marriage for many years, took domestic arguments to new heights. It was as if they regarded fighting as a natural progression in marriage. In the span of several years, they had obtained numerous warrants on each other for domestic disputes.

One Sunday afternoon I received a call to investigate a reported fight at their home in the projects. The dispatcher advised me that similar domestic calls had previously been recorded at their address, but it wasn't necessary. I was all too familiar with the Hunts.

As I coasted to a stop in front of their house, I could tell from the loud voices inside that the war was still raging. In the bushes surrounding a side window, two young children from the neighborhood were huddled together taking in the activities occurring inside. Hearing my footsteps, they sheepishly emerged from hiding.

"Hey, mister. Are you gonna put them in jail like on TV?" one of the kids asked. His impressionable eyes were wide with excitement as he jabbed his finger towards the house.

"Can we watch you point your gun at them?" yelled the second youngster, motioning towards my holster.

I stopped and looked at them for a moment, thinking about what they'd seen. Kids witnessing domestic violence is a disturbing matter. Not only are they constantly subjected to violence on television, but when they view it firsthand, their behavior patterns and acceptance of violence as a social norm is further enhanced.

"Nothing to see here, boys. I'm just going to have a little talk with them, that's all. Now you get on your bicycles and ride back home."

Heads hung in disappointment, they marched towards their bikes as I walked to the front door. I knocked several times before there was a pause in the commotion inside.

"Mrs. Hunt, I'm Officer Fielden. Did you call the police?" I asked as she pushed open the screen door.

"Yeah, and I'm mad, *damn mad*" It's that good for nuthin' husband of mine!" Jolene huffed.

If respect is linked to size, then Jolene Hunt deserved plenty of it. She was a large, powerfully built woman, with tangled brown hair that hung carelessly above her wide shoulders. Her sheer size made my 6'1" 220 lb. frame less dominating. While she stood in the doorway, I couldn't help but notice that the faded checkered apron surrounding her robust waistline looked as if it could stretch no more.

And, she was angry.

"I'm gettin' sick an tired of his mouth, an I told 'em not to call me them names no more!" she stiffly continued. She stood there like a statue, feet slightly apart, hands resting on her portly hips.

"Jolene, mind if I come in to talk?" I offered. She didn't reply, but simply inclined her head while slowly moving aside.

As I made my way into the living room, I saw James sprawled face-down across the sofa. Sensing my presence, he turned his thin body towards me, revealing a shallow gash

36

across his forehead. A narrow trickle of blood was slowly inching its way down the side of his face.

"All right, what happened *this* time?" I asked, sounding like a father about to scold his children.

"It's his fault, always is...we was in the bed, and he just got up and told me he was gonna kick my ass if I didn't turn off the TV and let 'em sleep," Jolene said.

"Hey now, *she's* the one that threw that damn ashtray at me, picked it up off the coffee table there and winged me right between the eyes, look here!" James innocently countered, pointing to his forehead.

"When, *just when*, is this going to stop? You all have been fighting like this way too long. If you can't live together in peace, it's time you thought about other arrangements."

My lecture was met with blank expressions, leaving me wondering if their marriage was indeed over, or simply on hiatus.

As with many domestics, it was rapidly becoming apparent that this was a no-win situation. The few minutes I was spending with the Hunts wasn't going to change the years of frustration and animosity which had infiltrated their marriage. An assault had occurred, and as upset as they both were, I felt the violence would probably continue if I left. My options were limited.

"Jolene, I'm afraid I'm going to have to take you in for assaulting your husband," I said.

"But *I* was the one who called the police! He said he was gonna kick my ass...hear me? Kick my ass. I can't believe that pint-sized excuse of a man..." her voice trailed off as she shook her head in disgust.

"You want to sign a warrant against James for threatening you?" I asked.

"You damn straight I do!"

37

"Well, James, looks like you'll be making the trip with us," I said, turning to face her bleeding husband.

I knew this wasn't the solution to their problems, but instead a brief pause in the action. However, it was the only step that could be taken in order to prevent further harm from occurring to either one of them at the time.

Unfortunately, this cooling off period for the Hunts did little else than give them a short reprieve from one another. It was only a matter of days before business was back to usual at their address, and I was heading over there once again.

Working some domestics can be similar to rearranging the deck chairs on the Titanic. No matter what you do, the end result is still the same.

"Unit 12, 10-57 (fight in progress), *112 Car-Mol Drive."*

The call came through as I was sweeping beads of sweat off my forehead. It was a hot August evening; the humidity in the stagnant air surrounded Nashville like a wet blanket. I had only been on duty for a short time, but was already feeling like I'd been put through a hot sauna while encased in Saran Wrap. This, along with hot summer car seats, can do amazing things to one's mood.

All in all, it was one of those nights that make people uncomfortable enough to cause their tempers to flare without undue provocation. It's almost a sure bet on evenings like these, we wind up responding to an abnormally high number of domestic incidents as a result of the weather.

When I arrived at the address, a thin, grandmotherly-looking woman met me at the sidewalk. The gray dish-apron she wore was torn at the shoulder; her raspy voice quivered while she tried to compose herself enough to speak.

"Thank God you're here. I'm the one...I called you," she uttered with a voice full of fear. "My sons are in the house, and I'm afraid they're going to...to kill each other!"

"Right now you're my first concern. Are you hurt?"

"I'm...all right, I guess," she said, nervously pulling the torn strap back over her frail shoulder. "Please, *please*...you must do something about my boys!"

After again assuring me she wasn't injured, I left her standing next to my cruiser while I hurried towards the house. I entered through the backdoor and found Ernie, the oldest, swaying unsteadily on his feet in the kitchen. His shirt was ripped open, exposing a pair of dark bruises on his chest and rib cage. The smell of alcohol drifted towards me as he struggled to catch his breath.

"*I'll get her for calling the cops, that bitch!*" he yelled the moment he saw my uniform. Slamming his fists on the counter, he quickly turned, and started to walk out of the room.

"You're not going anywhere or getting anybody," I replied, stepping forward and grabbing his arm. "*We're* going outside and get this straightened out."

I led Ernie down the sidewalk and onto the street between my cruiser and another patrol car which had arrived. He screamed at his mother with each drunken step, threatening he would "get her" for calling the cops. She stood in the distance, softly sobbing at her son's intoxicated remarks.

We soon learned that an argument earlier in the afternoon had stoked Ernie's fire, causing him to assault his elderly mother several hours later. He apparently had a history of unstable behavior, and incidents others would merely shrug off would cause his violent nature to surface. Fortunately, his brother was home at the time and was able to subdue Ernie before their mother was seriously injured.

Since neither his mother or brother wanted to have an assault warrant taken out on him, we could only charge Ernie with disorderly conduct (this event took place prior to the enactment of the updated domestic violence law). Ernie thrashed violently as we cuffed him, ignoring our repeated requests to relax and cooperate. Despite the turmoil he had caused his mother, she issued one final plea while we loaded him into the back of my cruiser.

"Please take care of him. Don't let him get hurt. He's really not a bad person."

Sometimes a mother's love for her children has no limits.

A half-hour later, Ernie was standing in front of the night commissioner (who, in the absence of a judge, determines probable cause to maintain someone in custody). At this point, most people tend to straighten up and present a better attitude, unless they enjoy the prospect of staring through a cross-section of cold metal bars overnight. Ernie, however, wasn't "most people."

"You all don't have any right to mess with other people's affairs! I'll kill the old woman, you just wait and see!" he screamed at the commissioner.

The commissioner lowered his head while Ernie raved on, as if to tune him out. Slowly arching his eyebrows, he peered over his glasses and frowned at the pathetic sight in front of him. "Put him in holding."

On cue, a deputy jailer stepped next to Ernie, and together we escorted him to the holding area. The moment we placed him into the cell, Ernie's anger manifested itself into a crescendo once again. Driven by internal rage, he screamed in fury while slamming his body against the metal doors blocking his escape.

"Where you guys going?" he shouted as we left him. "You all afraid of me? You'd better be, cause I ain't forgetting this!"

Had he been present, the Tasmanian Devil would have meekly spun off in search of quieter surroundings.

After filling out the necessary paperwork, the jailer and I walked back to the holding cell and escorted Ernie down the hallway to be fingerprinted. Muttering to himself about how badly he was being treated, he abruptly turned after we rounded the first corner in the corridor and started to walk away from us. I immediately grabbed his right shoulder, catching him in mid-stride.

"Police brutality!" he hollered, glancing over his shoulder to see if anyone was watching. "I've been thrown against the wall and choked! Get your damn hands off me!"

Everyone in the adjoining office snapped their heads our way upon hearing the words "police brutality." A momentary hush fell across the room; the gentle humming of a teletype machine was the only sound heard for several seconds. Then, seeing the young man's claims were unfounded, everyone quickly went back to their tasks at hand. I stood facing Ernie for a moment, wondering how he could justify abusing his mother, but when a cop grabs him, he yells "brutality" like a crazed banshee.

After fingerprinting, the jail accepted Ernie as a prisoner. Thinking I was finally rid of his high-decibel raving, I picked up my reports and headed towards the door. Two feet from the exit, however, one of the jailers caught up with me.

"Hate to tell you this, Fielden, but I'm afraid your boy's demanding to see a doctor. Says you kicked him in the chest, and now he's spitting up blood."

"That's bull-"

"I know," he interrupted, sensing my reaction. "We saw him chewing on his tongue to make himself bleed after we moved him to another holding cell. But still, he wants to see a doc."

41

It ain't over 'till the fat lady sings, and she hasn't even be-gun warming up backstage yet. The worn-out quote started ringing through my head like a bad dream.

I wound up taking Ernie to General Hospital, where he cussed, yelled and screamed the entire way. As we rolled down the highway, his shouting grew loud enough to drown out the dispatcher's voice on the radio. I found myself debating which could be worse...put up with his continued raving, or listen to someone drag long, ragged fingernails across a chalkboard.

Once we reached the hospital, Ernie made his thoughts known to everyone. *"Damn cops broke into my house and now they're trying to kill me! No son-of-a-bitch hassles me! I'll kill all of you!"* he cried out as a hefty male nurse lead him to an examination area. I followed closely behind, watching each step Ernie took.

"You seen the moon out tonight?" the nurse nonchalant-ly asked.

"Can't say I have," I replied.

"Full moon. Didn't even have to look outside to know. Makes two things happen you can always count on. More ba-bies are born during full moons, and it brings out the crazy in people. Toss in all the humidity outside, and you've got your-self a circus."

"So I guess that makes me the ringmaster tonight," I re-sponded.

"Yep. Full-moon madness, that's what we'll have to-night," he grinned as he penciled some notes in a chart.

While the nurse began to examine Ernie, I turned my back for a moment to look for a phone. Within seconds, Er-nie's verbal assault, again in full gear, suddenly took on a higher range, approaching that of a soprano. I spun around in time to see the nurse's stout arms wrapped securely around Er-nie's flailing shoulders.

42

"Those fists were getting too close to my face. Wife hates it if I come home in worse condition than when I left," he smiled through his thick beard.

This "bear hug" momentarily calmed Ernie down. Catching his breath, he reluctantly admitted that he had been a resident of Central State (a local mental institution), and he wanted to go back. Having said that, he glared at the nurse and refused any additional medical treatment. "You gotta name?" Ernie growled to the nurse.

"Mike."

"Well, touch me again, *Mike*, and I'll kick you so hard you won't have to cough during your next physical," Ernie sneered as he locked his arms across his chest in defiance.

"That's it then. We're gone," I said, picking up my paperwork. "Thanks for your help, Mike."

Mike shrugged his stout shoulders. "Hey, it's all part of the job...for both of us."

He was right, I reminded myself.

As we were leaving the emergency room, Ernie cautiously peered over my shoulder while a mischievous smile took control of his face. Seeing Mike was no longer in sight, Ernie's right foot snapped out and kicked the exit door off its track. It was, to him, an act of revenge.

He laughed at his achievement, but not for long. He was soon fighting in protest as a security guard and I grabbed his squirming body and carried him to the patrol car as a result of his unruly behavior. Moments later, Ernie and I were headed back to jail where he would be held on the original disorderly conduct warrant.

Some say cops look at the world through tinted glasses. These individuals need to realize that in police work, you constantly meet people at their worst, so you become conditioned to expect the worst in people.

43

It's all part of the job...for both of us, Mike's parting words echoed through my mind as I drove into the shadows of the full moon.

Catastrophe can strike when you least expect it. Precautions can be taken, but you can never completely eliminate the possibility.

When responding to a domestic call, you never know for sure what you're going to face. It could be a heated argument between lovers where demeaning words are the main weapon of assault, or a simple disagreement between a married couple that has snowballed into a physical confrontation. All thing considered, there's never really such a thing as a "routine" domestic.

Besides the inability to solve the problems at hand, another reason officers dislike domestic calls is the potential for one of them to turn into a 10-55 (officer in trouble) situation. Although this rarely happens, the consequences can be tragic.

I had been on the force for about two years when I was first confronted with such a call. It was about seven o'clock one summer evening, and I was nearing the halfway point of an otherwise uneventful shift. I was looking forward to grabbing a sandwich and catching up on some paperwork when the usual radio chatter was interrupted by the voice of a somber-sounding dispatcher.

"All units, 10-55 officer down, Litton Avenue."

A numbing chill raced down my spine as those dreaded words sunk in. My partner (who left the force soon after this incident) and I stared at the radio in silence while the information came through. The same anxiety and sense of urgency blanketed our faces simultaneously. A fellow officer was hurt, and they needed help...quick.

We were in Bordeaux at the time, around five miles from the call location. With sirens and emergency lights blazing into the night, we roared down Trinity Lane at full throttle. The anger, the concern building inside me quickly overwhelmed my thoughts.

God, please let them be all right.

As we turned onto Gallatin Road, we were greeted by a multitude of blue lights in both directions, reflecting around the traffic which had abruptly halted. When a 10-55 is broadcast, it goes out over all channels and *everybody* responds.

Several ambulances and other patrol units had already arrived on the scene by the time we reached Litton Avenue. A mixture of uniformed individuals darted about the street, busily securing the scene, redirecting traffic and shouting orders to one another. Through the flurry of activity taking place in front of us, my attention slowly drifted 50 feet to the left where two paramedics were standing over a body concealed under bloodstained sheets. Several officers milled close by, their hollow stares revealing an ugly truth. A fellow cop had been slain.

"All units, reported suspect in the 10-55 is a male black, early to mid-fifties, last seen wearing blue jeans with a tan jacket. Suspect is believed to be on foot in the Litton Avenue area, and is considered armed and dangerous."

I vaguely heard the dispatcher's voice, but my mind was unable to comprehend the words. It had blocked out everything other than the sight of the red-soaked sheet covering the man lying on the ground.

My fingers instinctively fumbled across the dash towards the radio. *Find the killer now, grieve later,* I thought while requesting dispatch to repeat the suspect's description. I then joined the other units in a search grid formed to comb the

45

entire neighborhood. Not long afterwards, one of our teams located the suspect and took him into custody. It wasn't until after our shift was over did we learn the sombering events leading up to the tragic evening.

Officer Billy Bowlin was walking up to the front door of a house in response to a domestic call, a routine he had performed dozens of times in his career. As Billy stepped onto the front porch, the suspect, crouched behind a bush 30 feet away, emerged with a scoped rifle and shot Billy in the head, killing him instantly. Billy never had a chance to try and reason with his assailant, or even to defend himself.

Billy's partner that night later described to a jury that Billy's head "exploded like a pumpkin" the instant he was shot. The death penalty was subsequently declined by the jury, and the convicted murderer was sentenced to life in prison. At his trial, his employer (representing a major corporation in Nashville) stated the accused was a good employee, and they wouldn't hesitate to hire him back.

A person murders a police officer, and the company he worked for thinks he has qualities good enough to hire him again.

Billy was a policeman's son, and I know his family was proud of him. He was a good cop. His superiors recognized him many times over for his exceptional devotion and bravery. His love for his job, his wife and family served as an example to all those around him.

His funeral was one befitting a fallen hero. Blue lights rotating slowly in somber despair lit the highway from over 300 police cars in the procession. Citizens even lined the streets of Gallatin Road as we went by, showing their respect.

My wife, Darlene, rode with me and provided what comfort she could. As we drove in silence among the procession, I struggled to fight back the tears filling my eyes. It was no use. You see, Billy wasn't just another fellow officer that I casually knew. He was like a brother to me, just like a member of my own family.

Sometimes it just doesn't make sense. We live in a society that has banned the sale of lawn darts because they are considered "dangerous", but almost any individual can purchase a high-powered rifle which can be used to kill any number of innocent people who just happen to be "in the way".

There are times when sharing part of someone else's life adds significance to our own. Those fortunate enough to have known Billy can understand this.

The police force lost a good officer that fateful summer evening. More importantly, however, the world lost a good human being.

Your memory will live on inside each of us who knew you, Billy. We'll never forget you, my friend.

And to the alleged human being that took him away from us...*damn you. Damn you to hell.*

4

CAN'T BUY ME LOVE

Money may not be able to buy you love, but you don't have to look around very many corners to rent it by the hour.

Prostitution is generally regarded as the world's oldest profession. Since the beginning of recorded time, people have exchanged an unusual assortment of goods and services for sex. As a matter of fact, the same sexual services once obtained by trading two chickens and a rooster are now available for around twenty bucks in most places.

Given this scenario, no police department is naive enough to believe they can completely wipe out prostitution. It would be like trying to nail Jell-O to a wall...it just can't be done. Instead, most departments try to control it to the extent where it doesn't become more widespread and readily available. If efforts weren't made to curb prostitution, it wouldn't be long before a number of these "flaming mattress kittens" would be advertising their wares to passing motorists by hiking their dresses up over their heads in monetary passion.

There are those who genuinely feel prostitution should be legalized. They reason that if it can't be stopped, then a system should be established whereby prostitution is taxed and regulated by the state (an approach which bears striking resemblance to the arguments used to end prohibition in the 1920's).

The theory behind this position is that the money exchanged for sex would be a taxable business transaction, which would create a larger tax base and resulting revenue for local governments. Also, by regulating prostitution, those involved in the trade would have to submit to frequent medical exams and be required to carry a health card certifying they are not infected with any sexually transmitted diseases, which would reduce the risk of disease exposure to the non-suspecting customer.

Finally, *in theory*, much of the crime associated with prostitution would be curtailed. This would lessen the time and resources (not to mention tax dollars) the police must commit to investigating these activities, allowing them to become more efficient in other areas of law enforcement.

If the whole concept of legalizing prostitution sounds preposterous, make sure your next vacation plans include a stop over in selected areas of Nevada, where legalized prostitution is alive and well. Within this land of casino riches and neon dreams, prostitution is taxed, regulated, and *heaven forbid*, the fundamentalists' protest, even advertised. If you're looking for some personal aerobic lessons, just flip through the local entertainment guide and you'll find full page ads for various bordellos, complete with seductive pictures of attractive escorts (as they prefer to be called at this level of entertainment) with accompanying rate cards.

Tennessee, like virtually every other state, has not subscribed to this "liberal" approach. Prostitution is illegal, and is covered under several laws.

In Davidson County, the local ordinance covering prostitution states that it is against the law for a known prostitute to be in a public place for the purpose of enticing prostitution. To understand this broad definition, bear in mind prostitutes have the same right to walk down any street they choose, just as everyone else does. It's only when they start flagging down cars and striking up conversations with potential customers that it is considered soliciting.

Many people can't understand this differentiation, and they call to complain whenever they see potential prostitutes strolling down a sidewalk, fully expecting the police to either arrest the women or make them go elsewhere. It just doesn't work that way. There isn't any crime in walking down the street...even in a short skirt, spiked heels and braless top.

A violation of any local (metro) ordinance is not a jailable offense, so if a prostitute is charged with a metro violation, they don't have to post a bond; they are simply given a court date and released. For that reason, most prostitutes are charged on an arrest citation, which is basically the same as being arrested without having to go to jail. If they appear before a judge to contest the charge and a guilty verdict is rendered, they're usually charged the maximum fine of $62.50...an amount they can easily recover in an hour or two back on the streets.

The state law covering prostitution essentially states that it is unlawful to promise any sex act for compensation. A prostitute can (but seldom does) receive jail time under this law. To get a conviction on this charge, you have to prove a certain sexual service was offered for a specific price. Officers in uniform, for obvious reasons, are generally unable to make cases of this nature. Most charges under the state law are made by undercover officers, who can solicit the prostitutes directly.

To understand why the police even bother arresting prostitutes, you have to look at the whole picture. We receive numerous complaints each year from business owners concerning prostitutes harassing their patrons or because used syringes and condoms have been discarded on their property. Added to this, the health department frequently requests our assistance in locating particular prostitutes after their customers become infected with a sexually-transmitted disease. Also, it's not uncommon to drive down a dead-end street off Dickerson Road and find a car parked on the side with a prostitute and their customer eagerly engaging in an anatomy lesson.

Over the years I have compiled a departmental pictorial guide used to identify convicted prostitutes who conduct business along the infamous Dickerson Road area of Nashville. Most of these ladies aren't a pretty sight; they bear the features of a rough and tormented life. Their inviting smiles often hide discolored rotting teeth, many smell rancid and few bear any resemblance to the pretty young girl who lived down the block from you in earlier years.

Some of these prostitutes undoubtedly carry the AIDS virus, and others have been brutally murdered. Sadly, a number of these women will continue to disappear from the pages of our booklet as they fall prey to their own choice of existence.

The majority of prostitutes I'm familiar with are drug abusers, and the main reason they sell themselves is to buy something they can snort, inhale or inject. They don't necessarily enjoy what they do, and do only what is necessary to support their habit. Many of them are armed, and being con artists, they would just as soon rip off their customer as to provide the services negotiated.

As such, it's not unusual to receive a call from a disgruntled male claiming they've been robbed by a prostitute. Once they learn the magistrate isn't likely to issue a robbery warrant in their case, but instead charge each party with prostitution, they usually lose interest. Still, there are some who are unable to see beyond their initial anger and remain mad enough to insist that the women be arrested anyway. For those few, I often allow them to place the prostitute under citizen's arrest, then transport the unlikely couple to the magistrate. The "victim" usually winds up winning the battle only to lose the war once discovering they are charged with prostitution as well.

The one bit of advice I can give to anyone interested in "sex-for-hire" is *caveat emptor*...let the buyer beware.

Make no mistake about it. Prostitution is a business. Pure and simple. And like most businesses, adaptation to changing market conditions is not only necessary for long-term growth, but for short-term survival as well. Case in point: despite the ominous specter of AIDS looming close by, prostitution activities, albeit with a few changes, are still going strong.

The prostitutes who don't respect the dangers of their profession and continue to market their services using unsafe methods will ultimately be "out of business." Some prostitutes have at least acknowledged the risks of their trade and now require customers to use condoms, even when engaging in oral sex. Astute prostitutes do this for two reasons. Foremost, it has become a matter of survival for them. Secondly, they know that in the time it takes to earn $40 performing straight sex once, they can service four customers orally and score double the previous amount.

Never let it be said that American ingenuity and the quest for efficiency has been lost to the Japanese.

The district I patrol includes the lower section of Dickerson Road, which is one of the two main areas in Nashville where people congregate to pick up prostitutes. You can find any type of potential customer there--young and old, married or single, professional people, thugs...the list goes on.

Around noon each day, a constant stream of customers settles into a holding pattern on Dickerson Road as the drivers search for their favorite selection. The prostitutes themselves are not hard to find; they spend several hours each day walking the streets and standing on corners waiting to be picked up. Most of the customers are interested in the traditional menu offerings, but sometimes the requests can get a bit strange.

I was assisting the vice-division with a prostitution sting at a local motel frequently used by prostitutes to conduct business. During this three-day operation, over 125 people were arrested for soliciting prostitution within a 50 foot strip in front of the motel. For every five minutes our female decoys stood on the sidewalk, an arrest was made. What makes this so incredible is that the decoys weren't flagging down customers. They were just standing there.

The customers ranged from their early 20's to late 60's. They were both men and women, black and white, armed and unarmed, local and out-of-state characters. Among those charged were a pharmacist, a local college head-basketball coach, an engineer, a minister, a milkman, a retired banker, a truck driver, as well as several college students. At one point the motel manager, sensing an opportunity for quick cash, approached our decoys and demanded a share of their "profits."

The sting operation was set up using an old, but nonetheless effective method. The decoys were wearing a wireless microphone while standing outside the premises, and I was parked nearby with a portable radio tuned to the same frequency. If a decoy was able to make a deal for sex, she would instruct the potential customer to drive around to the back of the motel and park in front of a particular room. Hidden behind the motel were several vice officers, who would then arrest the unsuspecting customer.

I was in an unmarked car, and my job was to help vice stop the customers that initially solicited our decoy, but then drove off after abandoning the deal. One gentleman, apparently short on cash, offered to trade her a bucket of chicken for oral sex. Whether this would have been the original recipe or extra-crispy, I never did find out.

Another customer was a young man driving a new sports car. His well-groomed looks and expensive clothes were straight out of a fashion magazine, giving me the impression he belonged on the set of *Beverly Hills 90210* instead of *Dickerson Road 37207*. His appearance could have gotten him an enjoyable evening with most any woman he desired...at least until the moment he whispered his special fantasy.

"Would you spank my bare buttocks with a Ping-Pong paddle for twenty bucks?"

Our decoy stepped back in surprise as he leaned over the seat to make his offer. I stopped him a few blocks down the street, and as he sheepishly emerged from the car, I spied a Ping-pong paddle on the passenger's seat, ready and waiting for action.

Prostitution remains one of the few occupations not requiring a resume.

It's been said that humans are the most intelligent of all species known to man. As a cop, however, you sometimes wonder about the validity of this statement after witnessing certain actions.

I received a call one afternoon involving a young male acting disorderly at a motel where prostitutes are known to conduct business. When I arrived on location a maroon Yugo, the cutting edge of Serbo-Croatian technology, was rapidly moving in the opposite direction towards the motel exit. I glanced at the driver as the car passed by, and noticed he didn't have anything on...at least from the chest up.

I turned my cruiser around and stopped him at the edge of the parking lot. As I approached his car, it became clear that the young man was completely naked.

"A little cool to be driving around without any clothes, isn't it?" I innocently asked, trying to hide the small grin appearing on my face.

"Well, uh...guess so," he stammered. He shifted embarrassingly in the seat as he spoke, trying to make the thin seat belt somehow cover his "particulars."

"Those your clothes in the back seat?"

"Yes, sir."

"Put them on and get in the back of my car," I said, shaking my head in disbelief.

Once dressed, I escorted him back to my car amidst the curious glances of onlookers. While he finished lacing his shoes in the back-seat, he started to tell me what had happened.

"Look, I never wanted any trouble, just a good time, you know. Hey, we're both guys, you can understand the certain needs a man has for a woman, can't you?"

I made no attempt to answer.

"Anyway, I was at the market about a block down the street," he continued, "and met up with this blond whore, and the two of us decided to come to this motel. When we got inside the room she told me to fork over twenty bucks and to take off my clothes so we could get to know each other better. Soon as I stripped down, she said she'd be right back, and walked out the door with my cash."

"Didn't you get a little suspicious?" I asked.

"Started to, right about the time this big dude came in and threw me outta the room. Hell, the sumbitch didn't even gimme a chance to put my clothes on! I beat on the door for awhile, but nobody would answer. It ain't fair...I want them arrested!" he exclaimed, apparently convinced he hadn't done anything wrong.

Our conversation was interrupted by the dispatcher getting back with me concerning the information I had requested earlier on the young man. His face turned pale as she relayed that he had an outstanding warrant for parole violation.

"Looks like you're out of more than just twenty dollars today," I said, turning to start the engine. "Besides what's happened here, I'm going to have to take you in on the outstanding warrant charge."

"What about the girl and the big dude!" he bellowed in disbelief. His eyes were fiery red, his nostrils flared with anger as he spoke.

"They're long gone by now. You've just learned an expensive street lesson, pal. It's best not to mess with a bull... you might just wind up getting stuck with its horns."

It wasn't long after this that a call was dispatched as a nature unknown, occurring on one of the side streets just off Dickerson Road.

When I arrived, a group of people were standing around watching an older fellow argue with a young prostitute. On

57

the curb behind them was a new Bronco 4x4 with its front end embedded in a concrete retaining wall.

I had just begun talking with one of the bystanders when the older man, who appeared to be in his late fifties, approached me. He was a round, burly soul with a balding scalp that towered high above his thick mustache like a pinnacle. His eyes were blood-red, partially from his intense anger, but mostly from the alcohol he had consumed. Barely able to contain himself, he breathlessly described his version of the situation, waving his arms with excitement in an effort to drive his point home.

"Look what she did to my truck! My new truck! I haven't even made the first payment on it yet!" he screamed.

"Listen, just calm down and-"

"I hired that girl over there to have sex," he interrupted, eyes narrowing as he jabbed his finger towards the prostitute, "and gave her a twenty, which I thought was fair considering her looks, but she decided she was worth forty more!"

The scantily-clad girl he pointed to looked as if she couldn't care less about what was going on. With a feigned look of innocence, she shrugged her shoulders and turned her back towards us while taking a long drag off her cigarette.

"I made the mistake of opening my wallet in front of her," he continued, "and when I pulled out the twenty, she saw all the money I had stuffed in there. That's when she raised the damn price. When I told her she wasn't getting any more, she got pissed off and started yelling I was a cheap son-of-a-bitch, then grabbed the steering wheel and swerved us into the wall!"

His anger over the damage to his truck overwhelmed him so much that he didn't realize he was admitting his own guilt to soliciting prostitution. Since his statement was freely given before there was any actual interest in him, the confession was used to obtain a prostitution conviction against him, as a specific act and dollar amount was mentioned.

The lesson is simple. When marinating in your own testosterone, never let your angry hormones speak for you. They make terrible lawyers.

"Unit 12, we have a 10-50 (theft) *reported,"* the dispatcher's voice filtered over the radio. It was just after sunrise and a steady rain had been falling for several hours. A ghostly mist hovered above the rain-soaked grounds, drifting across the highway like a scene from a low-budget horror movie. The hypnotic movement of the windshield wipers had taken my attention from the radio, and I instinctively jerked at the recognition of my call signal.

Still wet from working two earlier traffic accidents, I wasn't looking forward to stepping from the confines of my cruiser just yet. Murphy's Law of policework was beginning to take effect...the worse the weather gets, the more you can count on being out in it.

The address of the reported theft belonged to a run-down trailer park adjacent to Dickerson Road. Of the two dozen or so trailers located there, perhaps only a handful were fit to live in. The owners of the park had long ago decided it wasn't profitable or worth the effort to maintain their property, and as a result most of the trailers exhibited numerous signs of neglect. Their dented metal shells were speckled with rust emerging through creases in the paint, cracked windows were held together with duct tape, and the landscaping was nothing more than broken asphalt driveways running parallel to cinder block underpinnings littered with junk.

Still, it was home to the people who lived there. Not necessarily by choice, mind you, but it was the best they could afford on shoestring incomes.

Although some may pity them, we cannot dismiss them.

I pulled into the park and walked up the decaying wooden stairs outside the complainant's trailer. It was rented by a young girl named Carrie Ann, a street prostitute I'd given numerous solicitation citations to in the past. Carrie Ann was about twenty, but her deep-set eyes and narrow cheekbones gave her the appearance of being somewhat older. She was a polite, soft-spoken girl with sandy-blond hair and trim figure which made her popular with her clientele. The fact that she occasionally hooked across the street from her mother's house, where her baby was kept while she solicited business, was never a concern for her or her customers.

Carrie Ann was one prostitute I always felt a certain sorrow for. She wasn't too bright and possessed little common sense, as evidenced by the way she would hang around street corners where everyone could see her talk at length with potential customers, which is something most prostitutes avoid if they like to keep from getting arrested. Having very little self-respect as well, she solicited sex up to a month before she gave birth to her child.

Upon hearing me pull up, she met me at the door and invited me inside her dimly-lit trailer. The heavy smell of potpourri engulfed my senses as I stepped through the doorway, giving me the impression she was either overdoing the attempt to rid musty odors inside, or trying to mask the remaining scent of certain drugs recently used.

"Haven't seen you around in awhile, Carrie Ann. Hope that means you finally gave up the street life," I said. My attention gravitated towards the needle punctures in her left arm, and the gray, worn out veins running from her elbow to wrist.

"Yes sir, Officer Fielden, don't do that no more," she softly replied as she shifted her gaze to the floor. She stared intently downward, as if suddenly intrigued by her toes. It reminded me of how a child would react when caught doing something they weren't supposed to. We both knew she wasn't telling the truth, but was instead giving the answer I wanted to hear.

"I understand you want to report a theft," I began, deciding to switch the subject. "Tell me what happened."

"I just got home from my new job at the restaurant, and when I went into my bedroom to change clothes, I saw my clock/radio was missing."

I was glad to hear she had gotten herself a real job. Hopefully, it would be the first step in getting her life straightened out. Still, by the looks of her arm, she had a long way to go.

"Is there anyone else besides you that has a key to your trailer?"

"Yeah, my brother does. And...he's probably the one who ripped me off."

"What makes you think it was him?"

She shrugged slightly. "Believe me, I know him, and know he probably stole it."

I told her I would list him as a suspect, and left her trailer assuming that was pretty much the end of it for the time being.

The next morning Officer John Jordan and I responded to a domestic fight call at a hotel on Dickerson Road. As we walked through the front entrance into the lobby, a muffled cry from the registration area caught our attention. Behind the counter a young lady sat slouched in a chair, face cradled in her hands, while two staff members attempted to comfort her. When we approached the group, the distraught woman looked up for a moment, bringing into full view the aftermath of a severe beating. Her left eye was nearly swollen shut; the top of her pink blouse was smeared with the blood wiped from her bruised nose.

She regained her composure long enough to tell us that she had just begun her morning shift at the hotel when her boyfriend, Marty, angrily stormed in and beat her for no apparent reason.

"Did you all have a fight recently?" I asked.

"Not really," she whispered through the washcloth she dabbed across her cracked lips. "He's just a...a real jerk sometimes. He's too jealous, takes things so personal. Doesn't understand me, you know. He and his sister, Carrie Ann, can be-"

"Carrie Ann...Carrie Ann Beals?" I interrupted.

"Yeah."

I quickly related to John the events which happened at Carrie Ann's trailer the day before. I wasn't sure if, or how, they all tied together, but the focal point seemed to be Marty.

"What kind of car does Marty have? John asked.

"Doesn't have one. He can barely afford his smokes, much less a car payment," she replied.

After assuring her we would do whatever possible to locate her boyfriend, John and I began cruising the nearby vicinity. If he hadn't hitched a ride with someone, there was a decent chance we might find him in the surrounding area.

We soon located a suspect fitting Marty's description walking on the road shoulder several blocks from the hotel. He was tall and lanky, around eighteen or nineteen, with stringy black hair that fell below his narrow shoulders like the unkept mane of a horse. Covering his thin frame was an oversized T-shirt with one sleeve rolled up to hold his cigarettes. He looked like he didn't care a great deal for himself, much less for anyone else.

We pulled over several yards in front of him, cutting directly into his path. "I need to see some identification," I said, stepping from the car.

He halfway glanced over his shoulder and eyed me with disdain. His lips slowly parted as he began to speak, revealing discolored brown teeth that looked as if he'd just scarfed down an entire package of Oreos without milk.

"Don't have none. Kinda hard to pack a wallet in these torn pockets," he smirked, pointing to his ragged jeans. "But the name's Marty Beals."

I could feel my temper rising as he spoke. For a man to resort to physical violence when arguing with a woman, or for the strong to abuse the weak always infuriated me. If it's a fight someone wants, let them challenge a person of equal size and strength. Not someone who can't defend themselves.

"I'm placing you under arrest for aggravated assault, Marty," I said as John and I firmly placed him in the cruiser. "And while we're at it, maybe you can tell us something about your sister's missing radio."

"Oh, I can explain *that*," he interrupted. "I didn't steal it. I just pawned it for fifteen bucks so I could get me some cocaine. I went over to Carrie Ann's last night and shared it with her, so she's not pissed off anymore."

I made a mental note to bring this up with Carrie Ann the next time I saw her.

"And I *suppose* you can also explain why you beat up your girlfriend?"

He nervously looked around as if to determine if anyone else could hear what he was about to say. He then reached up to his collar, his hand slow and hesitant, and uneasily tugged at his frayed shirt.

"I, uh, kinda caught her in bed with someone else."

"It's one thing to get mad, but it's another to beat a woman senseless because of it. Are you such a tough guy around

63

someone your own size?" I shot back. The visions of the beating his girlfriend took were still fresh in my mind.

"You don't understand, man!"

"I don't see anything to under-"

"But I caught her in bed with another woman!"

My jaw dropped open as I looked at John, whose eyes rolled back into his bead. Silence took over the car while we headed towards the station.

Granted, I can understand him getting mad at what he saw, but beating her up for her actions can't be justified. Besides, it probably made her appreciate men that much less.

Sometimes there's a very fine line between love and vengeance.

5

VISIONS OF MORTALITY

HELP WANTED: Individuals to serve and protect society. Ability to work with the public in a friendly, caring manner a must. Potential candidates should not get easily discouraged at futile endeavors, or a possible loss of life, limb or property. Inquire within.

Someone once said that death is just nature's way of telling you, "check, please." If that's the case, I'm not quite through running up my tab just yet.

When you're a cop, you leave home every morning, knowing you might not come home that evening. It's part of a job description not everyone can adjust to.

The monster is real, and it doesn't lurk in the closet or under the bed anymore. It rides with you everyday, becoming a silent companion that patiently waits for an opportunity to nudge your senses.

Getting injured or losing your life in the line of duty is a demon all officers learn to face. It's not necessarily something you always fear, but rather something you are constantly on guard against. The statistics relating to this read like a ominous warning: During a recent 12-month period, over 38 Nashville officers were fired upon and more than 150 officers were injured in assaults. Nationwide, in 1990, a total of 150 police officers died in the line of duty.

In their own private manner, most police officers acknowledge the potential dangers of their jobs. They respect the risks in a way where they can be put into proper perspective, then tuck these thoughts away in their minds so it doesn't

65

overwhelm them to the point where it hinders job performance.

After all, fear causes hesitation, and hesitation can cause your fears to come true.

Although police work may fall somewhere between demolition experts and stuntmen on the "unsafe occupations" list, cops aren't put out on the streets totally unprepared to deal with hazardous situations. Through training and experience, you learn to minimize the dangers to others while striving to maximize your own safety.

Not all forms of training have proven beneficial, however. Keep in mind that the way you are trained dictates the way you'll react in a situation. When you go through a repetitious motion hundreds of times, it becomes second nature to apply new instinctive responses to a given situation without conscious thought.

Such was the case when "saving the brass" at the firing range was heavily emphasized. Instead of littering the ground with empty cartridges during target practice, officers were taught to automatically catch and pocket the bullet casings ejecting from their pistols. A habit was born. This practice was quickly discontinued after a couple of officers in a northern state were found clutching empty bullet casings in their hands after being killed in gunfights.

A day on the streets can be full of unexpected surprises. Routine calls may turn out to be dangerous, and seemingly dangerous calls may wind up being routine. To prepare for the unexpected, you learn to be careful, to keep your mind open and always stay on the defensive. Most of all, you try to never, *never* underestimate anyone. It can prove to be fatal.

Perhaps the most unnerving of all situations is when you find yourself alone with an armed suspect, and suddenly everything you do either counts for or against you. All too often the "rules" don't apply in these situations, and decisions hinging on life and death must be made in the blink of an eye. In the end, guts will only get you so far before they get you killed.

It's times like these, when you realize it's just you and a pistol along with whatever courage you can summon up to enforce the law, that shiny metal badge pinned on your chest can feel mighty thin.

The morning of September 8th began as most days usually do. The 6:30 roll-call was short and upbeat; several officers who had watched the program *"Top Cops"* on television the night before were energetically assuming the role of armchair quarterbacks while describing to anyone within earshot how they would have reacted in similar situations.

After receiving copies of the current criminal activity report for our zones, we headed out to the parking lot for a few last minutes of story-swapping. The subject of a recent TV talk-show, "businessman by day, transvestite by night," was being debated by several officers who were convinced the featured guest resembled a local entrepreneur. Since I didn't have a dog in that race, and my stomach was growling from missing breakfast, I passed on the conversation and headed towards my cruiser.

By 7:15, I was patrolling the east side of Nashville, armed with a steaming White Castle sausage and egg biscuit, and was ready to face the streets once again.

Or, so I thought.

An armed robbery had just been reported in the downtown area. Shortly after a description of the car and its tag number was broadcast over the radio, Officer John Tankersley located the suspect vehicle while circling a run-down motel just beyond the downtown business district. Seeing that one of the suspects was still in the car, John immediately called for back-up. I fielded the call and told him I would be on the scene within a minute.

Not wanting the suspect to flee, John meanwhile approached the car and ordered the driver out at gunpoint. The suspect took one look at John and spun out of the parking lot like a bat out of hell, barreling through the concrete blocks and chain link fence shielding the motel from the street.

I had just passed the motel and was about to turn into the lower side of the parking lot when an explosion echoed from behind. Spinning my attention to the rear, I caught a glimpse of the suspect's car as it catapulted out of the parking lot and through the fence, sliding sideways while crashing onto the pavement directly behind me. The sound of rubber scorching against asphalt splintered the air from both our cars as I slammed on the brakes with the force of my entire body weight. Everything loose in my cruiser ricocheted off the dashboard and seats as if shot from a cannon from the sudden change in momentum.

All this happened in a fraction of a second. If I'd been going a little slower, our cars would have collided, killing us both.

Managing to momentarily regain control of his car, the suspect swept passed me and rapidly accelerated down the street before swerving left onto Douglas Avenue. Unable to control his speed, however, he overshot the corner and slid into the side of a building six feet from the road. As the right side of his car hit the brick wall, he came to an abrupt stop.

I veered onto Douglas just as the grinding sounds of his transmission settled into reverse. Seeing the car's back-up lights come on, I knew there was only a few seconds left to act.

My mind was racing; I still hadn't shaken off the effects of almost being sideswiped moments earlier. A blur of options flashed through my thoughts, each being struck down as fast as they appeared. There wasn't time to wait for back-up and I wasn't close enough to confront him personally. As the suspect's car lurched backwards, the only chance to take him down became clear.

I quickly slowed my cruiser, then released the pressure on the brakes while grabbing the safety belt, making sure it was secured. Locking my hands onto the steering wheel with a vice-grip, I braced myself for the inevitable. A split-second later the sickening crunch of metal ran through my body as I rammed the suspect's car from behind.

The force of impact wasn't hard enough to injure him, but just enough to wedge his car into the building so that he couldn't escape. His disorientation from the collision would only last a moment. I had to take advantage of it quickly.

I jumped from the cruiser and positioned myself between the door and the driver's compartment, with my right leg braced on the inside floorboard. I leaned at a slight angle so the car's engine block would provide extra cover in case the suspect fired in my direction.

"Out of the car! Hands where I can see them! Now!" I yelled, jerking my .38 from its holster.

The driver's door inched open, but the suspect didn't make any effort to get out. Instead, like a snake coiling up to strike, he slowly turned so his head and upper torso came into view.

"I said move out of the car, hands out in the open, and I... mean...NOW!" I shouted over the blistering sounds of my siren, which was still running at full pitch.

My attention was darting between the view through the back windshield and the half-open doorway on the driver's side. As he remained motionless, I noticed his left arm was stretched across the front of his body in an awkward attempt to hold something out of sight. Although I couldn't see what was in his hand, *I knew, just knew,* it was a gun.

My chest began to tighten. Adrenaline pounded throughout my veins as every nerve-ending in my body tingled over the possibility of a lethal confrontation. The siren blasting next to my right ear was causing my head to throb, making it difficult to concentrate. *Easy now, don't force it to happen 'til you're ready,* I mentally whispered to myself as a clammy sweat formed between my palms and gun.

The suspect rotated his head just enough to glance in my direction from the corner of his eyes. Sizing up the situation, his left shoulder slowly began arching backwards.

"Make one sudden move and I'll drop you where you sit!" I yelled as he leaned towards the door.

I took in a deep breath and squinted my eyes, tracing an imaginary line from the barrel of my gun to the suspect. As I tightened my grip on the pistol and pulled the slack out of the trigger, I felt the cylinder start to rotate to the next firing position.

This is it. He's gonna go for it, and I'll have to waste him. Why won't he just give up? Is he really willing to die over some stolen money? Still, if he drops quickly and gets off a couple of shots, I may be the one who gets hit. Can't give him that chance. Hope I don't miss him this close. Dammit! Should've grabbed my shotgun instead of the pistol!

From a distance, the alternating pitch from a second siren began to mix with my own. Another patrol unit was headed our way. My eyes didn't waiver; my complete attention remained locked on the suspect. If he was going to make his move, it would have to be now, before back-up arrived, and we both knew it. Inching my way to the left, I shifted into a half-crouched position to get a better shot...and waited.

He didn't flinch. Within moments, Officer Jana Buse pulled next to my cruiser. The calvary had arrived.

The gun was growing heavy in my hands as sweat gathered around my collar. Renewed confidence filled my voice as I again yelled at the suspect to get out of the car. He continued to sit there for a long moment, pondering his next move. Finally coming to the conclusion he was outmanned and outgunned, he emerged from the vehicle.

"On the ground, spread eagle!" Seeing my pistol aimed dead-center on his chest, he dropped to the ground in despair, a frustrated street-warrior who had come to the realization that his battle was beyond hope.

I abandoned the protection of my cruiser and sprinted towards him while Jana provided cover. "Move an inch and I'll kill you, plain and simple," I whispered next to his ear as I jerked his arms behind him and cuffed his hands.

After putting him in my patrol car, I went over to search his vehicle. In the floorboard on the driver's side, confirming my suspicions, laid a loaded 9mm pistol. Near it was a small bag of cocaine, which he tried to stuff under the seat before surrendering.

Hindsight is a great thing to have, especially if you're aware of it beforehand. Unfortunately, it usually doesn't work that way. Still, I'm convinced he would have shot me had I approached his car after stopping him. Already having an outstanding parole-violation warrant, he knew the additional charge of armed robbery would likely send him back to jail for the rest of his life. Shooting a police officer probably wouldn't have made much difference to him.

Although my involvement in the whole ordeal was less than ten minutes, it left its mark on me. My voice was reduced to a hoarse whisper from yelling over the siren; the adrenaline which flowed through my body minutes earlier had dissipated, leaving me exhausted. Everything happened so fast. There hadn't been time to realize how scared I was until it was all over. Minutes before, I was handing the cashier at

71

White Castle a couple of dollars for breakfast, and moments later I narrowly avoid being torpedoed in the side by a 2,000 pound Chrysler hurdling through the air, and come dangerously close to killing someone at gunpoint.

Times have changed, and it gets more hazardous on the streets every year. Given the popularity of cocaine and crack, many criminals are heavily armed and have little regard for human life. Instead of cheap weapons like the old Saturday Night Special, many of them now carry the firepower of magnums and uzzis. It's getting to the point that their arsenals make ours comparable to stone knives and bearskins.

Not long after this incident I purchased a 9mm and retired my .38. I wanted to have the comfort, perhaps even the "psychological confidence booster," of having a 15-round clip instead of the traditional six rounds. It all boils down to when you're tossed into a situation under fire, you never know how efficient you'll be in reloading until you actually run out of ammo. Easy tasks on the practice range can become a fumbling, unnerving effort when the pressure is on.

The majority of patrol officers in Nashville now carry semiautomatic pistols as well, the Austrian Glock 17 being the most prominent model. In addition to the aforementioned reasons to change, perhaps the biggest drawback to the .38 caliber lies within the cartridge itself.

I recall one night when several robbery detectives reported shots being fired while pursuing a suspect they had armed-robbery warrants on. Moments later, the detectives radioed that the suspect had wrecked. I was the first patrol unit to arrive on the scene, and immediately upon seeing the condition of the suspect's vehicle, I knew whatever fight he may have had in him left the moment of collision.

He was slowly twisting himself out of the driver's side window when I pulled up. Considering the damage to his car, he wasn't in too bad of shape. Although groggy, he was alert enough to realize what had happened.

"Oh, man, I'm hurtin'...get me outta here," he moaned. As my uniform came into focus, he shook his head. "Guess I'm shit outta luck, huh?"

"No, actually you're in luck...you're still alive and in fairly good shape," I said while patting him down and cuffing him. He offered no resistance as I placed him in the back of my patrol car. After I had settled into the front seat and informed dispatch the suspect was in custody, he started to complain.

"Oh man, I've been shot...they shot me in the back! I can feel myself bleeding!" His voice rose with each word as if suddenly realizing he was about to meet his maker.

Not seeing any blood around his waistline when I searched him, I was skeptical. Still, by procedure, I had to check out his claims. I pulled him from the rear seat and leaned him up on the side of the car.

"I'm gonna die, you all killed me!"

"The only thing you're going to do is go to jail," I replied as I stretched his shirt up over his left kidney, where he indicated he'd been shot. We both looked down at his side and saw a small red mark, where a .38 slug had apparently passed through the thin metal car door and exhausted its energy when it hit him, unable to penetrate the skin.

"Remind me to find you a Band-Aid when we get to the station," I said, raising an eyebrow with mock concern.

His jaw muscles twitched for a moment as he sighed a breath of exasperation. While not letting the seriousness of the situation escape him, he permitted himself a grim smile.

"Yeah, and I guess you'll be needing to get me a lawyer, too."

*   *   *   *   *

Like a number of police officers, David Littrell worked a part-time security job in order to supplement his income. He was employed by the Starlite Club, a relatively nice nightclub that my wife and I would sometimes visit for a relaxing evening. The Starlite is known for its hospitality, country music flair and seldom has any problems involving the patrons.

One evening David came across two men in the process of "permanently borrowing" a Buick Regal from the Starlight's parking lot. As he approached one of the men and ordered him to freeze, the suspect spun around and shot David in the chest, sending a .38-caliber bullet through his heart. Even though he'd been hit, David managed to return fire and wounded his assailant.

The shooting was witnessed by a group of people walking out of the Starlite. Several of them ran back inside and located Joe Towers, another police officer at the club. Joe immediately called for assistance and within minutes ambulances and patrol cars were on the scene. David was rushed to Memorial Hospital, where he was quickly opened up in the emergency room. He miraculously survived.

In the meantime, the suspect David wounded stumbled in the parking lot while trying to escape. Three good-sized fellows quickly caught up with him and administered their own version of street justice by beating the living daylights out of him. The other suspect was arrested without incident after being spotted over a mile away by area residents.

David was fortunate. He has since recovered, and is now back at work with the police department. He almost lost his life that night while trying to protect someone's car. Somehow, the tradeoff doesn't seem right.

Officer Bob Gentry, a former veteran on my detail, is another example of how fate can be an unmerciful mentor, rearing its head without a moment's notice.

Bob was leaving the city garage one afternoon after running his cruiser through the car wash. As he headed west on Peabody Street, a Metro garbage truck traveling in the opposite direction made a left turn and accidentally plowed into the driver's side of Bob's car. The impact was so severe that it tossed his patrol car 25 feet, knocking the light bar off in the process. Bob suffered severe brain damage in the collision. The truck driver was uninjured.

To this day, Bob is still a patient at a head-injury treatment center in Florida. His wife used to bring him by the station every Christmas, but sadly, Bob never recognized any of us.

Car accidents injure far more officers than being shot ever did.

6

THOSE WHOM SOCIETY
DISMISSES

"Put some tape over my mouth if you want me to hush! I told you I can't stop talking...you've got to understand!"

Officer Monty Mendenhall and I had just entered the chapel of a funeral home in response to a disorderly person call. Directly in front of us was a small crowd paying their respects to an elderly husband and wife, who had passed away within days of one another. Up high and to the left an organist slowly swayed while playing "Shall We Gather At The River" to a somber audience. As the tune floated throughout the chapel, a crackling plea for help rose above stifled sobbing.

"I said get me some tape! Why aren't you listening to me? I can't quit talking...they gave me a truth shot!"

Just ahead on our right, a small group formed around a thin, fragile woman. Their attempts to console her were having little effect. As she nervously squirmed in her seat, her sobbing voice filled the air.

"Keep your hands off me! I'm not crazy, leave me alone!"

At first I thought she was just upset and that her behavior was a normal reflection of profound sorrow. After all, we had been told moments earlier that the deceased were her parents, so I could understand her anguish. But when family members told us she had a history of mental illness and had struck at several of them in the chapel, I knew her outbursts went above and beyond normal grieving.

"The truth serum is making me do this! Fetch me some tape, you hardhearted people!"

As the family parted to let us in the narrow aisle, Monty and I gently sat down on each side of the distraught lady. If we had to take her with us, I thought, I wanted to do it as quietly as possible...without having to drag her kicking and screaming over a pew. Emotions at the funeral were high enough already, and we didn't want to spark a situation which would turn anyone against us.

"Hello, Lillian. I'm Officer Fielden and this is Officer Mendenhall," I calmly said, motioning towards Monty. "What's making you so upset?"

"They called the police on me, I see," she viciously retorted. Anger burned in her swollen eyes as she slammed her hands into the lap of her black dress. "You don't understand, that's my momma and daddy lying up there! I seen the spirits rise from their bodies, just like I can see the demons in the people in here! Get me some tape so I can be quiet!"

As her family had tried minutes earlier, I attempted to calm her down and make her realize the commotion she was creating. However, I didn't have any more luck than they did.

"They killed my daddy with one of those things the ninja turtles use...no, I mean them things the ninja karate people use...I saw it myself! It could've been my brother, I saw him with one of them things! They just wanna get rid of me so they can have my house!"

"Lillian, it's going to be all right," I tried to assure her. "Why don't we go outside for some fresh air and talk?"

"I ain't going nowhere! Stay away from me you...*you monster!*"

Her family members quietly looked on with helpless stares as she continued to babble incoherently between sobs. I glanced at Monty, whose eyes darted between Lillian and myself, and wondered if he was feeling the same sense of awkwardness that I was. Her parents were dead, and we were about to be forced to take her away before she could lay them to rest. After vainly trying to reason with Lillian for several more minutes, it became clear we had to remove her from the premises.

I nodded to Monty, signaling it was time to break the impasse. We slowly stood up, raising her gently by the arms while holding her between us. No one in the chapel made any attempt to stop our efforts, apparently feeling the service would continue better without her. As we sidestepped down the aisle towards the front door, Lillian wailed in protest as she wildly thrashed her heels across the carpet. A sense of guilt washed over me when we passed by the minister, who clutched a Bible close to his chest while shaking his head in dismay. I resigned myself to the fact that we had no other choice in this situation, especially since the complaint was lodged by her son (who was possessed by the devil, according to Lillian).

Once outside, we eased Lillian into the back-seat of my cruiser. An unexpected hush fell over her the instant I shut the door. Grateful for the momentary silence, I turned to meet her approaching son while she sat quietly facing the window, casting icicle-like stares at us both.

"I apologize for the disruption inside. As you've seen, my mother has some problems," he said softly, stopping next to my cruiser. "This has been going on for some time."

He spoke with an attitude of indifference while providing us with the information for our reports. His behavior, considering what had happened in the chapel, was strangely void of all emotions. He acted like he'd been through this routine before with his mother and knew she needed the kind of help he couldn't provide.

"...and that's what led us to call the police," he said, gesturing helplessly towards his mother as he finished his explanation. The moment those last words left his mouth, Lillian erupted into an emotional frenzy once again and started hammering on the rear window with her tiny fists.

"Let me out now, *please!* I wanna go back in!"

"Quit beating on the windows and hush!" Monty shouted in return. The whole situation was frustrating both of us. In addition to the unsettling circumstances we had been drawn into, we both knew the procedures involved in taking someone to the mental hospital can often tie up several hours. This translates into two officers being out of service for that period, which spreads other patrols thin as they attempt to cover your zone as well as their own. The result is slower response times for burglaries, traffic accidents, domestics and whatever other calls may accumulate.

I thanked her son for his help as Monty and I got into our patrol cars and started towards Vanderbilt Medical Center. Their staff physicians would have to assess Lillian's condition before recommending admission to Middle Tennessee Mental Health Hospital. We had just rolled out of the parking lot when her screams began to echo throughout the car once again.

"Where's my purse! I want it back!"

"I've got your purse up here, Lillian. I'm going to hold on to it until we get to the doctor."

"I don't want to go to no doctor! I wanna see my momma and daddy! Please, *I beg you*, get me some tape for my mouth so I can go back in there!"

"Lillian, nothing would make me happier than for you to be able to go back in there and be with your family."

"You got no heart! You're going off with the demons, can't you see it? I know these things, I saw the possession leave my momma's body the night before she died!" she insisted as she started clawing on the screen between us.

"Lillian, listen to me now-"

"You've got to believe me, they're just trying to get rid of me in there, to stick me in some hospital with crazy people! I've seen the demons!"

"If you don't calm down and quit hitting the screen..."

"You might as well kill me! You're heading for Hell too, can't you understand?"

"...I'm going to handcuff you."

"You got no heart! Please, *don't take me awayyyy*!" Her raspy voice trailed off as tears overtook her words.

As I looked back at her through the rearview mirror, I began to realize that she looked much older than she actually was. Her wrinkled face reflected the years of internal torment which had slowly eaten away at her; the jet black hair she must have been so proud of in younger days now owed much to artificial measures, but still, the gray roots surging forth would not be denied. She lived in her own world, sullen and remorseful, one full of mistrust and imaginary ghosts, but nonetheless a world as real to her as the morning sun.

When we arrived at Vanderbilt Medical Center, I radioed dispatch a time and mileage check (a standard procedure when transporting a female, designed to provide documentation in case any claims of misconduct are filed against officers). By then, Monty had rejoined us, and the three of us made our way into the reception area inside.

After a short wait we were escorted to a private room for Lillian's initial psychiatric screening. She didn't seem to mind; as a matter of fact she had calmed down and was taking things quite well at this point. While we semi-patiently waited on the doctor, Lillian started to ramble on about her life, her family, people she knew who had "switched bodies" and whatever else came to mind. I occasionally nodded out of respect, and would sometimes toss in a question or two about what she was saying in order to keep her one-sided conversation peacefully rolling. Content with the fact that someone was actually listening to her, she continued on, seldom taking a breath between sentences.

After a lifetime of thirty minutes, the doctor finally arrived. Clipboard in hand, she rattled off a series of routine medical questions, to which Lillian cheerfully replied with lengthy explanation. Pausing momentarily to review her answers, the doctor then decided to run a psychological profile on Lillian.

"Do one of you need to stay with her during the interview?" she asked, turning in the direction Monty and I were sitting.

"Not him, he's the mean one!" Lillian interrupted, pointing to a suddenly bemused Monty. "He yelled at me awhile ago."

Monty wrinkled his brow as he looked around the room. He flipped his palms upwards, curled his lower lip, but said nothing. The *'who, me?'* look spread across his face was response enough.

I grinned at the thought of how overpowering first impressions of Monty could be to those who didn't know him. As a weight-lifter, his broad frame stretched the confines of his uniform to the limit. His cleanly-shaven bald scalp revealed a hint of his renegade spirit, which was further enhanced by a small hole in his lower earlobe that, on duty, was vacant of the earring he wore while playing in his band on weekends. Monty's a good cop, and apparently to some, an intimidating one as well.

We both decided to wait in the hallway until the doctor was finished. An hour later, the physician emerged from the room and told us she would be notifying Middle Tennessee Mental Health for admission. Her diagnosis was that Lillian suffered from paranoid schizophrenia and chronic non-compliance. As she turned down the hallway, I looked back into the room and saw Lillian sitting upright and proud, still

81

emphatically talking...but this time there was no one to listen. She was alone.

Minutes later, Lillian and I were back in my patrol car. As Monty pulled in behind, we began our journey to Middle Tennessee Mental Health. Just as we merged into the traffic flow, she looked at me with a sudden expression of seriousness.

"Why didn't you ever stop at the store and get me some tape? It would've kept me quite, you know."

"Well, they were probably out," I replied. "It's getting really hard to find good tape these days."

"If you had any compassion, you would've at least tried," she answered while settling back into the rear seat, folding her arms across her chest in disgust.

By the time we pulled into Middle Tennessee Mental Health, over two hours had lapsed since we first responded to the call. While Monty and I checked Lillian in, she became more relaxed and at ease with the whole situation. Still talkative, it seemed she now felt this was nothing more than a chance to meet the kind of people she could somehow relate to. For her sake, I hoped so. She was a lonely, disturbed woman who needed companionship and support.

Once Lillian was settled in, I left the building and climbed back into my cruiser. I had just turned the ignition when an elderly lady, who appeared to be in her late eighties, gently knocked on my door. Rolling down the window, I was greeted by a warm smile and compassionate voice.

"Young man, I just wanted to tell you something that people should say more often," she began, leaning over an old cane. "I think you police do a wonderful job, and most of us really appreciate the work you do. I'd like to say a prayer for you if you don't mind."

As I looked at her in amazement, she laid her crooked hand feebly across my arm and began to recite a short prayer.

When she finished, she turned at me with her kind eyes and whispered "God bless you, officer."

I didn't know what to say except "thank you." I was caught up in the moment, for in the 14 years I had been on the force, that wonderful lady was the first person I'd met who went out of their way to pay tribute to a cop's job. I had long ago grown accustomed to the hatred and indecencies some people can display, but sincere acts of kindness was something I wasn't used to. During that one moment, I was reminded why I became a cop, and all of the resulting hardships suddenly became worthwhile.

Two hours earlier I was being cursed to the devil. Now, I was being blessed. As she hobbled away, I found myself hoping that when all the chips were counted, I somehow broke even for the day.

The call was on a demented male in a residential area near some government-funded apartments. It happened on a blustery winter afternoon, and although the temperature was hovering near 30 degrees, the biting wind chill made it feel much colder.

When Officer Suzanne McClure and I arrived, we spotted a young white male leaning against a car in the parking lot, gazing blankly into the sky. His clothing was disheveled; all he had on was a torn pair of blue jeans, a shirt unbuttoned down to his waist, a single, ragged shoe on one foot and a muddy sock on the other. Oblivious to the fact that we had pulled in next to him, he continued to focus his attention upward, as if waiting for something to happen.

"Tell us what you're looking for up there and maybe we can help you find it," I said, hoping to break the spell he was under.

He slowly lowered his head and looked in my direction, but at the same time gazed right through me. His red eyes swam in a clouded haze, giving me the impression he'd been staring at a television test-pattern most of the morning.

"Want to tell us your name?" Suzanne chimed in.

He blinked with forced effort, trying to bring her into focus. He then mumbled a few syllables we couldn't understand.

"Let's try it again," Suzanne encouraged.

"Bill Jon-sssshhhoo...," he slurred. Raking long fingers through his tangled hair, he summoned forth every ounce of coordination in order to stand upright.

As Suzanne started running variations of Bill's last name through records, his attention drifted towards the ground surrounding a row of nearby bushes. His eyes darted around for several seconds, then zeroed in on what appeared to be a rib bone from a small animal. He leaned forward, took one clumsy step, then let his momentum carry him to the shrubbery. He fell several feet short of his goal.

I got out of the cruiser and walked towards Bill as he crawled within reach of the bone. Seeing me coming, he quickly grabbed the thin object and stuck it between his lips. Somewhat pleased with his endeavor, Bill began to "puff" on the bone, thinking it was a cigarette. A contented grin spread across his pale face.

"Can I give you a light, buddy?" I good-naturedly prodded.

His reply was a vacant stare.

I glanced at Suzanne from the corner of my eye and saw her shaking her head in disbelief. We both felt he was under the influence of *something,* and rather than arrest him, we decided to try and get Bill some help.

We loaded him into our cruiser and headed to the nearest firehall. Soon after arriving, we located a couple of paramedics and convinced them to take a look at our new friend. Just as they began checking his vital signs, however, Bill's behavior took a turn for the worse.

"They're crawling all over me!" he yelled as the stethoscope hit his chest. "Gotta get the...ummmphh...aaahhh!"

The startled paramedics jumped backwards as Bill lashed out in terror. He screamed incoherently, throwing his fists towards anyone within reach, but his wild swings only connected with air. Everyone stood back in confusion as Bill's aggression abruptly shifted inward. Grabbing a handful of material, he ripped at his own clothing in a panic-stricken frenzy. Exhausting his energy within seconds, he collapsed back into a chair and quietly attempted to catch his breath.

Thirty minutes earlier, he had the personality of an exhumed corpse. Now, he made Attila the Hun look like a gentleman.

"Uh, look, we'd like to help, but this guy really isn't the kind of emergency case we're equipped to handle. Why don't you take him to a hospital?" one of the paramedics remarked.

"Guess we don't have a choice," I responded. As Bill returned to his tranquil state, Suzanne and I took him by the arm and led him out of the firehall.

Once rested, Bill's internal beast again surfaced as we neared the hospital. The car shook as he repeatedly slammed himself against the back door, driving his elbows against the window with the force of a hammer in an attempt to escape.

"Looks like we've got a regular Dr. Jekyll and Mr. Hyde on our hands," Suzanne frowned. "Maybe it'll help if we gave him another bone to smoke," I replied. She nodded, thinking I was kidding, but I was beginning to wonder if it wouldn't be such a bad idea.

For his own safety, we decided to handcuff Bill before he put his fist through one of the back windows in the cruiser. We pulled in behind a vacant building to do this, for if we had trouble cuffing him, we didn't want it to happen on the side of

85

a busy street.   Regardless of the circumstances, someone would have invariably misinterpreted the situation and would wind up calling in to complain how we "abused" Bill if he re-sisted our efforts to make sure he didn't injure himself during transport.

When we arrived at the hospital, the nurses weren't overly happy to see us after being greeted with the Mr. Hyde version of Bill's personality. Wisely sensing the disturbance he was about to cause, they promptly sent us back to a treatment area in the emergency room.

I stood next to him while he attempted to balance himself up on the examination table. As he slowly rocked back and forth to a tune only he could hear, a nurse realized he was wearing only one shoe. She looked him in the eyes and inno-cently asked, "Where's your shoe?"

By then, Bill was showing faint signs of coming back to reality. He looked at the nurse with a deadpan expression and matter-of-factly replied, "On my fucking foot."

Well, at least one was.

Another nurse placed a cup of liquid in front of him. "You're not going to like our refreshments, but you have to drink this. It will induce vomiting. Whatever you've taken has got to come out, one way or another," the nurse comman-ded.

He hesitated for a minute until the alternative, a rubber hose being forcefully inserted down his throat, was convinc-ingly explained to him. It didn't take Bill long to comply with the nurse's request after hearing that.

After listening to him regurgitate for several minutes, the nurses agreed that Mr. Hyde was finally in submission, leav-ing Bill too sick to cause any more trouble. Realizing there was nothing more we could do, Suzanne and I left.

As fate would have it, Suzanne saw Bill a month later while she was working an extra job at the same complex where we initially found him. After filling him in on the events which he was unable to remember, she asked him what led up to the ordeal.

"My old man always told me that gratitude is something only a dog shows," he replied. "Anyway, I appreciate what you all did for me. It was a stupid mistake. I almost overdosed from some drugs."

I haven't seen Bill since that day at the hospital, but I hope he learned something from his experience. Bill was lucky. Countless others die each year who don't get the second chance he did.

Some experts claim that over 50 percent of all crimes are somehow drug-related. *Over 50 percent.* Most of us who work the streets feel that percentage is way too conservative.

Think about it for a moment. Get rid of the drugs and drug dealers infesting our cities, and while we're at it, imagine cutting out the demand for them at the same time. All of a sudden crime rates are cut in half. A Utopian view, to say the least.

It's going to take a lot more than reciting "just say no" to accomplish this. The logic behind believing that these three words will magically make things better makes as much sense as telling a manic depressive to "just cheer up," or a kleptomaniac to "just put it back".

There's got to be a better way.

They are referred to by a number of generic names. Homeless, economically deprived, misplaced citizens, just to mention a few.

Beyond these well-packaged titles are the people who have fallen between the cracks in the system. A number of them once held decent jobs and contributed to society, while others cannot remember any kind of life except the one they now live.

Although their ranks are filled with those of varying races and backgrounds, they share at least one trait in common. They live in a nation that once proudly proclaimed "Give us your hungry, your poor, your tired and weak...,"

So, now that we've got them, what's the next move?

Dealing with the homeless is nothing new when you're a cop. And though many of their faces and stories may fade from memory, there are a few you just can't forget.

I received a call one afternoon to check out a report of a man asleep on Interstate 65. When I arrived at the location, I noticed a large, black male lying on top of the concrete barriers that separated the north and south bound lanes of traffic. How he could sleep there during rush-hour traffic was beyond me, but knowing that he would fall directly into a lane of traffic if he accidentally rolled off either side of the barrier, I knew it was time to interrupt his nap.

As I gently prodded him, his eyes began to flutter in an attempt to focus onto me. He then stretched out his massive hand and scratched the salt-and-pepper beard which hung from his cracked cheeks like an old mop.

"I'm...uh, my name's Horace. Hope I, um...I didn't cause you no trouble, officer."

He was somewhat disoriented, but I could tell he was making every effort to be sincere.

"No trouble, Horace. You just picked a dangerous spot to take a nap," I replied.

"Don't usually make a habit of this. Just got tired all of a sudden, you know. Reckon my body's older than my mind thinks it is."

"You live around here, Horace?"

"Been stayin' down at Union Mission, but got fed up with all the fights and riffraff hangin' round down there, so I decided to head back to Chicago."

He slowly sat up and stood on his feet. It was then I realized just how big he was, as I looked squarely into his chest. He was a giant, but a seemingly gentle one at that. I became thankful that when the good Lord made people this big, he sometimes gave them a kind disposition so they wouldn't make life miserable for the rest of us.

"Kind of a long walk to Chicago from here, isn't it?" I asked. "Why don't you let me take you back to the mission, or maybe to see a doctor."

"No, thank you kindly just the same. I'll be just fine. I've caused you enough trouble already." A tired, desperate smile spread across his leathered face as he spoke.

He began to straighten the torn flannel jacket he was wearing, as if to make it fit more comfortably. It was a futile attempt, for it was several sizes too small for his stout frame. Over his long pants was a pair of faded shorts held in place by a frayed belt. Like many others in his situation, Horace made do with what little he had.

After a few moments of conversation, I managed to convince Horace to at least let me take him to the closest exit off the interstate. He slowly nodded in agreement and then made his way into the back of my cruiser. Before he sat down, he reached into his back pocket and carefully unfolded a ragged newspaper and laid in on the seat underneath him.

"I'll try not to get your police car dirty," he said, shifting comfortably in the backseat.

I smiled inwardly. Here was a man who had nothing, who had few reasons to thank society for anything, and yet he was concerned with getting dirt in the back of my cruiser.

I let Horace off at a nearby intersection and bid him farewell after cautioning him to be careful. As big as he was, he was still no match for some of the cruelties people in his situation must endure. He graciously thanked me, then turned and slowly made his way down the street.

Later that evening, I was heading home from my part-time security job at the Rivergate Mall. Walking down the left side of the street was a large black man wearing a tight-fitting flannel jacket. I knew in an instant it was Horace. He had walked about three miles from where I had left him earlier.

The homeless have a saying: "No matter wherever you go...there you are." Those who can't relate to the kind of life these people struggle through on a daily basis have to think about that for a moment to understand it.

Wherever you are, Horace...I hope you made it to Chicago.

7

WHISKEY GETS THE BLAME FOR A LOT OF THINGS IT DIDN'T DO

It was a cool, crisp fall morning; the kind of morning Southerners welcome after a muggy summer.

The light fog from the night before still floated in the midst of the crimson-colored tree leaves highlighting the countryside. The damp air was quiet and still, the silence broken only by the rhythmic orchestration of crickets in nearby fields.

The serene setting gave no hint of the chaos about to erupt.

It was 5:30 a.m., and I was enjoying a scenic drive through the countryside enroute to the usual morning roll call when a booming voice broke through the low-level radio chatter. Its intensity sent vibrations across the instrument panel.

"All Units, this is Unit 16...my patrol car has just been stolen!!!"

I recognized both the patrol number and angry voice as those belonging to John Donnelly. Knowing how personal cops get about their cruisers, I knew he was mad enough to spit venom when he radioed in. It's one thing to have another officer mischievously hide your car when you step inside the station for a minute, but it's entirely different to have it driven off by someone *outside the department.*

To put it in a "non-cop" perspective, it's like a stranger borrowing your toothbrush.

I broke in on the channel and asked John his location. After determining he wasn't injured, I flipped on my blue lights and headed in the direction he said his hijacked cruiser was traveling. The picturesque scenery would have to wait.

As I darted down the highway, the events leading up to his misfortune began to unfold. John was heading towards the station when he came upon a single vehicle accident. When he got out of his cruiser to investigate, one of the intoxicated individuals involved in the wreck, a 17-year-old girl, jumped into his car and sped away.

The irony of the whole situation would have been amusing if not for the danger involved. After all, it's not everyday you get to chase a stolen police car down a major highway in Nashville.

The light fog from the countryside had turned into a dense mist by the time I reached Gallatin Road. Visibility quickly deteriorated as I moved down the highway, giving me the uneasy feeling of driving through a thick bottle of milk. As difficult as it was to pursue someone in these conditions, I knew the intoxicated girl behind the wheel of John's car was faring even worse. It would only be a matter of time before someone got hurt if we couldn't stop her.

Just as I slowed down to cross an intersection, I spotted the flashing blue lights of John's cruiser faintly cutting through the fog about fifty yards ahead. Either the teenager was too drunk to notice the lights were still on, or she simply didn't know how to turn them off.

I darted around the traffic to catch up with her before she disappeared into the fog once again. As I shortened the distance between us, she swerved off Gallatin Road and onto Riverside Drive. Seconds later, she lost control and ran off the road, crashing head-on into a large oak tree.

The cruiser's blue lights were still rotating, eerily reflecting off the fog and back onto the twisted wreckage when I pulled in behind the car. As I ran towards the vehicle, the severity of impact became frightening. The front end of John's cruiser was crushed like an empty beer can. Pieces of glass mixed with the radiator fluid flowing across the ground like a broken dam. I leaned inside the car, hoping she'd been sober enough to strap herself in before the accident.

Unfortunately, she didn't.

Her still body lay stretched across the front floorboard, her head and shoulders crumpled next to the bent frame of the driver's door. The smell of alcohol drifted close to her bloody face.

Be alive, dammit, be alive...

Reaching down to check for a pulse, I expected the worst. The moment my hand touched her neck, her ribcage slowly expanded. Although she was unconscious, I was flooded with relief to find she was still breathing.

"Unit 12, I have a 10-46 (vehicle accident w/injury) *on Riverside just off Gallatin Road. Request paramedic assistance."*

I slid the portable radio back into my belt and stood silently next to John's cruiser for a moment. The skid marks on the asphalt beneath my feet bore a grim reminder that accidents involving alcohol become a fool's explanation for destiny.

A breath of exasperation left me as I looked back at the young girl. The peaceful, contented mood I enjoyed earlier while viewing nature's wonders had been wiped away. It was back to business as usual.

Several minutes later the paramedics arrived. They removed the girl from the wreckage, started an IV after checking her vital signs, then quickly strapped her limp body onto a portable gurney and slid her into the back of the ambulance. Then they were gone, consumed by the fog as the wailing siren slowly faded into the distance.

It turned out that the girl was a runaway from a local children's home, having been placed there by the Department of Human Services. Her fun-filled night away from the state's custody had left tragic consequences. Upon her recovery, she would be charged with DUI and vehicle theft.

The message should be clear by now. Don't drink and drive. Get crawling, commode-hugging drunk at home if you want, but don't pour yourself into a car afterwards. If you do, sooner or later we're going to get you.

Especially if you steal a police car in the process.

*   *   *   *   *

Officer John Donnelly's cruiser after the wreck; Fielden surveys damage at rear of car.

Walking the line between your moral obligations and the legal responsibilities of being a cop isn't easy. There will always be incidents where certain circumstances must be considered and weighed against what remedies the legal system has to offer.

The streets are full of those who are sick, needy, mentally ill and homeless. Many of these suffering individuals have vainly cried out for help, but haven't received an adequate response from our social institutions. When these overcrowded and underfunded institutions fail, all too often it's the police that have to deal with the aftermath. And when this happens, our options are sometimes limited.

Late one afternoon a hit-and-run was reported on Trinity Lane. Although my shift was winding down, I volunteered to take the call. Supper would still be warm by the time I got home if this was a typical hit-and-run, since the reporting driver usually doesn't remember much more than the make and model of the second car involved, which reduces the time-consuming task of paperwork.

The vehicle forced off the road was a large pickup pulling a travel-trailer. The driver was standing next to his trailer, cursing at every moving object in sight when I coasted to a stop behind him.

"First day of my damn vacation and look what happens! Some hairball slams into my trailer and knocks me off the road. Did he care? Hell no, the guy just kept going! Next time I decide to see the countryside around this city, it's going to be through an airplane window!"

After venting his frustrations, he told me he was beginning to turn left on the highway when the car tailgating him tried to pass on the right. When the car came around, it sideswiped the right side of the trailer, causing a significant amount of damage to both vehicles in the process. The car then continued down the highway, its driver never stopping to see if anyone was injured.

While I was working the accident, another officer located the suspect vehicle several blocks down the road. The impact had been so severe it snapped the front tie rods of the car in half, leaving the wheels cocked at an odd angle. How he managed to maneuver down the highway in that condition was beyond explanation.

The person who caused the accident had abandoned the vehicle and was found several hundred yards up the highway. He was walking as quickly as possible in an attempt to distance himself from the wrecked car. His pace wasn't too fast, however, since the individual was 63 years old and had a crippling case of emphysema.

I finished working the initial part of the accident then drove to where the suspect was. He was sitting on an embankment when I arrived, wheezing furiously as he fought to catch his breath. He was a mere stick of a man, a frail shadow not weighing more than 85 or 90 pounds. When I asked him for his driver's license, he stroked a bony hand across the mountains of sweat rolling from his forehead onto his sunken cheeks.

"Ain't got one, mister. It's been revoked," he replied.

"For what reason?"

He struck a match and touched it to the cigarette propped between his lips. He gazed into the flame, slowly flickering in his hands as it burned down before answering.

"DUI"

I went back to my cruiser and called his name into records. They soon informed me that the elderly man had been charged with numerous DUI's, as well as driving on a revoked license. He also had a probation warrant outstanding; he had violated his probation terms on a previous DUI by being arrested for another DUI.

"Wish I'd been killed in that wreck. I'm gonna die anyway. Tired of waitin' for it. Wasting away to nothin', that's all there is to it," he gravely cried. Despair filled his hollow eyes while I helped him up and guided him towards my cruiser.

When we arrived at the station, I took him to booking where he continued to cough and gasp for breath. The walk from the parking lot wasn't over 30 yards, but to him it was like hiking a steep mountain in a thin atmosphere.

As we asked him the routine questions, he earnestly pieced together what answers he could from his fading memory. It quickly became evident that the years of alcohol abuse combined with his sickness had stripped him of much of his mental abilities.

During the questioning we learned he didn't have any living relatives or a permanent residence. Instead, he lived in his old car, parking it in a different lot each night as he traveled the highways that became his home.

I asked him if he was going to be able to breathe all right before locking him up. He nodded that he would, then refused my offer to take him to a doctor.

It was difficult not to feel sorry for this pitiful, worn out old man. However, he was the same type of person that winds up killing innocent people on the highways. It leaves you wondering what the solution is. Do you lock him up for the rest of his life, which may only be a matter of a few months? It seems cruel when you look at the individual, but there's a problem which has to be solved, a social dilemma the police department isn't equipped to handle.

What help society fails to offer, the courtrooms are left to decide. It then becomes a case of providing an imperfect solution to an imperfect world.

And in many cases, no one comes out ahead.

*   *   *   *   *

Part of the police function is to conduct tavern checks to insure the owners are operating within compliance of the laws relating to the sale of alcoholic beverages. Since the sale of these beverages represents the owner's livelihood, it's not unusual for them to cover up problems occurring inside their establishments which could jeopardize their operating license.

It was just after 8:00 one October evening when I received a call concerning a knifing victim near Trinity Lane. The area where the call originated was home to numerous dingy taverns, whose names seemed to change as frequently as the seasons pass.

I arrived on the scene within minutes. In the meantime, several people had already gathered near the young man that had been stabbed.

"About time the police got here. It'd be nice if they came the same hour they were called," someone sarcastically muttered as they stepped aside to let me through.

I bit my bottom lip hard enough to chew through it. No matter how often I heard foolish remarks like these, it's difficult to resist the temptation to fire back at someone. If people want quicker response times from the police department, they should be willing to pay the costs associated with hiring the officers needed to adequately patrol the streets. It's all a matter of economics...less funding means fewer officers which results in more backed-up calls. Mention a tax increase to cover the cost of additional officers and these critics quickly become silent. Everyone wants better protection, but no one seems willing to open their wallets and pay for it.

I redirected my attention to the young man lying on the sidewalk. Beneath his blood-soaked shirt were several stab wounds to his right chest and lower abdomen. Although he was sliced up pretty bad, it didn't seem any vital organs had been severely damaged. He was semiconscious; his hands were covered with the blood seeping from the wounds as he held his chest tightly in an attempt to keep any more fluids from escaping.

"Listen to me. You're going to be O.K.," I reassured him. "Try and tell me your name."

His lips moved slowly to form a single word, but no sound emerged. Frustrated at the attempt, he sucked in a shallow breath, eyes squinting in pain as he tightened the grip on his chest.

"Terry," he hoarsely whispered.

"Can you tell me where you were attacked, Terry?"

"Back...there, somewhere," he said, nodding to his left.

"An ambulance is on the way. Just hang tough and you'll be all right. You're going to make it, man."

I looked in the direction he had motioned and saw a bar about 30 yards to the left. After the ambulance arrived, I made my way over to *Zeno's,* a rustic tavern typical of the "hole-in-the-wall" bars of the area.

Walking into *Zeno's* was like stepping back in time. The dingy barroom looked as if it belonged to an era which had long since disappeared. The faded yellow linoleum floors were covered with cigarette burns and sticky beer stains. The obscure lighting from the few fixtures that weren't broken or burned out barely provided enough light to view the patrons inside. Off to the right, a tattered neon beer sign intermittently flickered to the sounds of a Hank Williams tune blaring from an ancient jukebox.

"What'cha want, blue man?"

The voice from behind caught me off guard. I spun around and was confronted with a short, pudgy woman who identified herself as the owner.

"I'm here to investigate a stabbing. A young man down the street has been seriously injured, and he indicated the attack took place near here."

"Don't know anything about it," she said, her face reflecting a look of boredom.

I glanced towards the small crowd circling the bar. They were a crusty bunch, a rough group of ragged souls who looked as if they spent most of their waking moments hunched over a bar cradling a mug of beer. Standing alone in the shadows behind them was a tall, bearded roughneck wearing biker clothes. He stood silently, slowly stroking the heavy chain he wore as a belt. One look told me he wasn't to be trusted out of eyesight.

"Does anyone know anything about a stabbing that took place around here a few minutes ago?" I asked to no one in particular.

The group of barfly's shook their heads and once again became entrenched in their drinks.

I thanked the owner for her time and headed towards the front door. Just as I was about to step outside, a small trail of fresh blood inside the doorway caught my eye. Stooping to get a closer look, I could feel the owner's stare cutting through my back.

"Looks like one of your customers left something behind," I said, still kneeling. "Think you best tell me where this blood came from."

"Don't have any idea. Maybe somebody cut their little pinkie on a beer tab," responded the owner. A chorus of muffled giggling erupted from the group around the bar at her comeback.

I was now fairly certain the stabbing *had* taken place there, but I needed more to go on. I decided to make a nuisance of myself until finding what I was looking for.

"Well, if that's the case, I'm sure you won't mind if I take a look around," I said.

Everyone's eyes locked onto me as I casually strolled past her to the bar. Stepping up to the railing, two ruffians

101

grudgingly moved aside to let me through while mumbling under their breaths. I knew I wasn't welcome there, and since good whiskey has been known to make a jack rabbit slap a bear, I kept a close watch on everyone in case someone decided they had enough testosterone to prove how tough they were in front of their buddies. Anger quickly feeds upon itself in a barroom crowd, and the addition of alcohol fuels hostile feelings even more.

Leaning over the battered railing, I saw several blood-soaked towels piled inside a trash can. To the left was a sink stained with blood, as well as the floor underneath it.

"Must've been a real nasty gash with that beer tab. You want to tell me what *really happened* now?"

The short woman leaned back on her heels slightly. "Don't know how that got there," she replied as she nervously began to fidget with her hair braid.

I walked over to where she was standing. By this time my eyes had adjusted to the hazy lighting inside, and I could tell by her glazed stare and alcohol-laden breath that she had hoisted one too many from her side of the bar.

She suddenly shifted one foot behind her, causing me to glance down. Traces of blood surrounded the heels on both her shoes.

"I've had enough of this. *Lady, there's blood on your shoes, in the sink and on the floor.* I want to know what happened here. *Now!*" I stared directly into her eyes, not moving an inch.

She hesitated a long moment before replying, unable to come up with any more lies. "Look, all right man, I'm sorry. Hey, just don't want no trouble with the *poe-lease,* you know. These two boys been drinking then all of a sudden they got into a fight. Before I could break it up, one got poked with a knife. I kicked them both out and that's all there was to it. I didn't call you blue men cause *I just didn't want no trouble.*"

My anger snapped like a rubber band. "You've gotten yourself into more trouble by trying to avoid it. A man could've *bled to death* down the street, but you didn't care about that. The only thing that mattered to you was saving your own hide."

I couldn't understand how uncaring one human could be towards another. Are we that fast becoming animals? If someone else hadn't called us, the young man probably would have died if he hadn't received medical treatment.

I knew the victim was going to remember that day for some time to come. I was going to make damn sure the owner did as well.

"I'm placing you under arrest for public drunkenness. Clear out your customers. I'm shutting you down."

"This is *my bar*!" she hissed. "I'm not outside, you can't do that!"

"You're in a public place and you're intoxicated. End of story," I said as I led her outside.

Arresting her on public drunkenness would be chalked up to "officer discretion." The key to proving a public intoxication case is the officer's testimony on how he determined the defendant was under the influence, such as the smell of alcohol, slurred speech, staggering, etc. Unlike DUI, there is no preset limit to the blood-alcohol level someone must legally have before being charged. If someone registers *any* alcohol, and appears to be under the influence, they can be charged with public drunkenness. And although the owner had the right to request a blood-alcohol test, she didn't exercise that option. Had she done so, she would have been responsible for the cost of the test, regardless of the result.

The next morning I went down to the Metro Beer Board and filed a complaint against *Zeno's*. Since several related problems had occurred there in the past, the board ultimately decided to suspended their license for 7 days.

I had no doubt that *Zeno's* would reopen again, perhaps under a new name or under new ownership. The names and faces may change, but the problems would, in all likelihood, still be waiting there for us another day.

It was late morning on Christmas Day. Instead of waking up to a white Christmas, Nashville had been besieged with a cold rain for several hours. The clouds were thick and gray, leaving a dark shadow stretching for miles across the city. Thoughts of snow-filled Christmas mornings I awoke to as a child in Knoxville filled my thoughts, making me wish the temperature would fall a couple more degrees so I could once again feel the security of those memories.

"Unit 12, 10-45 (traffic accident) *at 1227 Gallatin Road."*

"Unit 12 acknowledging...ETA 2 minutes," I replied.

Working traffic accidents is fairly common on rainy days, as many people simply don't take the time or exercise the proper caution to adjust their driving to slippery road conditions. Since most people were at home celebrating the day with their families, however, the streets were relatively clear of traffic which kept accidents to a minimum.

By the time I arrived on location, the middle-aged man involved in the collision had stumbled out of his car. Several yards behind him was a 1972 Grand Prix which had been introduced to a telephone pole. A cloud of steam was spewing from the car's radiator, covering the demolished front end with a thick mist.

"Are you hurt?" I asked the swaying figure.

"Nope!" The force of his words caused him to stagger two steps backwards as he spoke.

It was obvious that the driver had consumed a bit too much of holiday cheer. As he continued to wobble, I knew it would just be a matter of time before he fell flat on his face. I helped him over to a grassy embankment and told him to sit down while I called a wrecker.

"Phone pole...hit me," he tried to explain. He crossed his arms over his knees and buried his head under them as he began to choke back the tears.

On my way back to the cruiser, I stopped at his car to assess the damages. On the inside floorboard laid a small gift box which had been crushed upon impact. Next to it was an envelope with a snowman holding a large heart on the front.

I started to envision a scene minutes earlier, of him leaving home with his special gift for some loved one. Now, he sat on the ground crying, both his car and plans destroyed on Christmas morning.

A quick check on his driver's license came back without any prior arrests. After the wrecker arrived, I placed him in the back seat of my cruiser and started towards the station. My shift was almost over, and I was anxious to get home to my wife and kids for our Christmas celebration. I knew by now my children, Christy and Marcus, would be eagerly waiting at the door for me so they could open the gifts Santa had left them.

And then I started to think about what kind of Christmas the man in my back-seat, Mr. Average Joe with his clean record, would be facing in the drunk tank.

I turned off at the next intersection and headed away from the station. Ten minutes later, I pulled up to the address listed on his driver's license and led him up the sidewalk to his house.

"How can I...I ever thank you?" he emotionally slurred as we stood in the mixture of sleet and snow that suddenly appeared. He looked at me with red eyes while grabbing the doorway for support. As he did, a single tear slowly rolled down his cheek.

"You just did. Merry Christmas," I said, turning back down the sidewalk.

I got into my cruiser and glanced back at his house before starting home. He was still standing in the doorway, cradling the crushed package I had retrieved from his car. He meekly raised his hand and waved, then smiled for the first time since I met him.

That was all it took to convince me what I'd done in his case was justified. Had it been any other day, I would've continued on to the station and charged the man with driving under the influence, clean record or not. It's an area I don't cut much slack in. But, it was Christmas...and there's just some places a person shouldn't be on Christmas.

Behind bars for their first DUI is one of them.

8

LASSIE TO THE RESCUE

The collie sat high above the ridge, its unwavering attention focused on the events transpiring below.

It didn't matter who the strange people in the valley were, or why they were running through the woods. The important thing was that they may provide some food, or even a brief moment of companionship. But still, the collie sat transfixed, momentarily content to remain a curious spectator of the activities...

It was a late summer morning when I received a 10-70 (burglary in progress) call from the Whites Creek Pike area. A rash of burglaries had plagued the vicinity in recent months, and since I lived close by, I jumped at the opportunity to catch whoever was responsible.

I was soon joined by Garry Baker, the officer who normally patrols the Whites Creek zone. As we sped down the highway in tandem, the dispatcher advised us that a neighbor had seen two male juveniles pull up in a red Blazer and force open the front door of the residence. I asked the dispatcher to keep the informant on the phone so we could stay updated on the activity inside the house. Since Whites Creek Pike extended close to the county line, I also requested the Robertson County Sheriff's Department be notified in case the suspects fled in their direction before we arrived.

The morning drizzle, which had been nothing more than a minor nuisance since dawn, turned into a downpour while Garry and I accelerated down the interstate. By the time we approached Whites Creek Pike, the rain took on the intensity of a thousand tiny jackhammers and slammed against our windshields with such a force our wipers were rendered useless. I found myself leaning forward, forehead resting inches from the windshield, as if being closer to the cascading sheets of water would somehow make it easier to see through it.

As we neared the call location, the dispatcher alerted us that the neighbor continued to monitor the suspect's movement from next door. They had already taken two loads of merchandise to the Blazer, and were currently back inside the house. I signaled Garry, and we switched off our sirens in order to remain inconspicuous as long as possible.

The reported address was a small split-level brick house approximately 75 feet from the road. As we coasted to a stop in front of the driveway, the red Blazer came into view. Seconds later the silhouette of a young man appeared at the front door. He took two steps outside before looking up and spotting our cruisers. Startled at our presence, he immediately slid to a stop on the wet concrete porch, tripping over himself as he dropped the box in his hands before retreating back inside. He moved so quickly, the only detailed feature I could make out through the heavy rain was that he was wearing white tennis shoes.

Not the ideal suspect description to file on a report, I thought as I jumped from the cruiser.

Pistols drawn, Garry and I bolted towards the front door. The yard was damp and soggy, tugging at our hard-soled shoes with each step. We hit the front porch with a muddy slide and quickly positioned ourselves on both sides of the door. While we paused a moment to catch our breath, I could feel my soaked uniform drawing up around my body. Unable to absorb any more water, it clung to my skin like a tight latex glove. I thought of our raincoats back in the cars, where they were doing us a lot of good at present. In our haste, we hadn't bothered to put them on.

I eased around the doorway far enough to take a quick glance inside. Seeing no movement, Garry and I cautiously moved through the entrance. In the middle of the hallway was a pile of entertainment equipment the suspects had been in the process of loading into the Blazer when we arrived.

While we conducted a room-by-room search, an occasional thumping sound echoed throughout the house. Winding our way down the hallway, we soon located its source. The door on the back porch was swinging from its hinges as the wind swept it to and from the doorway. The suspects had escaped.

The moment Garry and I stepped outside, we stopped dead in our tracks. Directly in front of us loomed several hundred acres of dense forest. Garry muttered something unintelligible while inching his clinched chin in the direction of the wooded area. I nodded in silent agreement. This wasn't going to get any easier.

We knew sooner or later the suspects would emerge from the woods onto one of the streets which ran perpendicular to Whites Creek Pike. However, since we couldn't possibly cover every point on the highway, we would have to find them while they were still roaming around in the forest.

We quickly dismissed our first two search options. There wasn't time to bring in the closest K-9, who was on the other side of the county with an on-call officer at home, and the bad weather made it hazardous to fly surveillance in a helicopter. It would all come down to a lucky crapshot that we, along with additional search teams, could find the suspects by securing the perimeter before they had a chance to escape. In the process, hopefully someone would catch sight of the twosome as they scrambled through the woods.

Within 20 minutes several other Metro patrol cars arrived, followed by a state trooper and a Robertson County deputy. After a quick meeting to coordinate our search patterns, everyone fanned out into their assigned zones. Fifteen minutes later, Sergeant John Lyle spotted the suspects running north through a small clearing before disappearing back into the heavy brush. With the odds now breaking in our favor, we had to move quickly before the pair strayed deeper into the woods.

Officer John Jordan and I piled into a cruiser and headed down a mud-laden path towards an abandoned trailer approximately 1000 feet from the road. Our car buckled at every hump along the way as thick mud surrounded the wheels, making it almost impossible to navigate around the narrow trail.

As our cruiser settled into the ooze of the overgrown yard surrounding the old trailer, we caught a glimpse of the two suspects huddled in the brush just beyond a rusted barbed wire fence. From a crouched position, they peered between the 20 yards of bushes separating us, unsure if we had seen them.

It was then we were joined by an unexpected back-up.

I had just stepped out of the car when a rustling in the underbrush from behind startled me. Spinning around, I quickly unholstered my revolver, halfway expecting to confront the Swamp-Thing. Instead, grinning from ear-to-ear, a collie bounced into view.

The dog playfully trotted over to the cruiser where John and I were standing. Despite its matted, burr-encrusted hair, the collie was full of energy. Vying for our attention, he began to romp in circles around us.

"Hey man, don't sic no dog on us! Don't turn him loose!" came a frantic plea from beyond the fence.

"He...he won't bite, will he?" interrupted another scared voice.

Wanting to take full advantage of the changing situation, John didn't hesitate a second.

"He will if I tell him to," he replied. As John winked in my direction, a mischievous grin took control of his face. "Haven't fed him since yesterday, so he's getting kinda hungry now, if you know what I mean."

Our new recruit couldn't have cared less about what was going on around him. Starved for attention, his only concern was figuring out ways to get us to pat him.

"No second warning, guys. Ya'll come on out now, or I'll have our dog come in and get you," John threatened.

That was all the suspects needed to hear. They ambled over the barbed wire fence, then stood out in the open for a moment, each prodding the other to make the next move towards or away from us.

While the pair debated their next fateful step, the dog began to whine. From the corner of my eye, I could see him sprawled on his back, legs dangling above his body in hopes that someone would scratch his belly.

"Lassie! Prepare!" I yelled to the collie.

Hearing a loud voice, the dog rolled onto his feet and turned in my direction, its ears jumping to attention.

Whatever thoughts the suspects may have had in fleeing left them that very instant. They hesitantly approached us, keeping their eyes fixed on the collie with each cautious step.

"On the ground, face down, hands behind your back!" I instructed them. Like two well-trained marines, they quickly stretched out in ground formation.

Meanwhile, the dog had come to the realization that John and I were too busy to give him much attention. Giving up on us, he wandered over to the suspect I was cuffing and began to lick him across the face.

"Get the dog off me! He's eatin' me alive!" The young man yelled in horror as he jerked his head away from the collie.

While the dog stood there, confused over the reaction to his friendly nuzzle, I laughed. Sometimes, life is good.

"Maybe we should deputize the collie," I kidded John as we led the young men to the car.

Once in the back-seat, they freely confessed to the burglary. They told us they had been on their way back to Kentucky from Myrtle Beach, South Carolina when they ran low on gas. Out of money, they broke into a house in order to fund their journey home.

As it turned out, the juvenile court in South Carolina wasn't too happy about this. Since the Blazer had been taken during a robbery in their state, they wanted their "kids," ages 16 and 17, back for questioning.

If I ever doubted that a dog could be man's best friend, I'll doubt it no more.

At least not until a cat shows me it can strike fear in the hearts of criminals like the collie did that afternoon.

Well done, Officer Lassie.

9

A FAMILY AFFAIR

To provide their families with a decent standard of living, extra jobs become a routine practice for police officers. Besides the additional income, the advantage of working 60-70 hours a week is that you're too tired to get into any trouble when you're finally off the clock.

There are, however, some drawbacks associated with carrying a part-time job. For example, employers often feel you should do whatever they wish, even if there is a conflict with police department policy. Also, you wouldn't be needed by the employer if there weren't any problems in the first place.

These drawbacks can come to a head when an incident occurs during an off-duty job. Let's say an employer demands you take a certain action during a specific situation. You follow through with their request, then wind up finding your efforts aren't supported when the employer claims you're an "independent contractor" after a lawsuit arises. The resulting court time and expensive legal assistance become issues you may have to tackle on your own.

I've worked hospital security jobs for almost nine years. Fortunately, the supervisor of the firm I work for is a police officer as well, which has helped to minimize potential problems.

Hospital emergency rooms can be the equivalent of Pandora's Box. You never know what type of patient will walk, roll or crawl through the door next. One minute, the doctors are treating someone with a sore throat, and the next, they're attempting to resuscitate a gunshot victim. The mayhem generated within these walls can set the stage for a roller coaster of emotions. It's these emotions, misplaced as they sometimes are, that can lead to some unusual confrontations.

"Security, report to the ER," a nameless voice over the intercom hastily instructed. Noting a sense of urgency in the call, I retired the half-eaten chicken sandwich I held to a nearby trash can.

As I rounded the corner leading into the emergency room, I saw a young lady shifting uneasily in a wheelchair in front of the reception area. Directly behind her stood two young men, one of whom was profusely arguing with a nurse.

"We don't have time to register her, lady! We need to see a doctor, *now!*" his angry voice boomed through the waiting area.

"If you'll just calm down and take a seat with your brother," began the nurse.

"Don't tell me to calm down," interrupted the young man, "my wife is about to bleed to death!"

During this exchange, his wife sat in the wheelchair with her face buried in her hands, too embarrassed to say anything. She appeared to be eighteen or nineteen, and wore a simple plaid dress which contoured her rounded state of pregnancy.

"Tyrell, if you'll shut your mouth and let the lady do her job, maybe we can see the doc," spoke the other young man.

"Ain't your concern, Kevin! Now back off!" retorted Tyrell.

Silence took over the crowded waiting room as everyone focused their attention on the heated exchange taking place before them. Knowing this bad situation was about to get worse, I moved in between the two brothers.

"I think the three of us need to have a little talk. Let's step outside a minute while they get the young lady registered in," I said.

Tyrell's head snapped up immediately, his voice dropped a tone lower in register. "Not until we see the doc," he growled through clinched teeth.

I realized Tyrell was on the edge, and was about to lose whatever control he had left. "She'll see a doctor soon," I assured him. "You've gotta understand this commotion is just going to slow everyone down. The quicker we go outside, the faster she'll be taken care of."

The logic seemed to stick. Breaking off their vulture-like stares at each other, Kevin and Tyrell reluctantly shuffled through the exit doors along side of me.

Once outside, I tried to reason with Tyrell. I told him that his wife would receive any medical attention she needed, but I wasn't going to allow him to cause any more disturbance in the emergency room. His choices were simple. Either shut up or leave the premises.

Hearing this, Tyrell's mouth opened for an instant, but no sound came out. Instead, his cheeks flared out like a blowfish as he began taking rapid, shallow breaths, fueling the rage which grew wild in his eyes. The volcano was about to erupt.

"I'm not going to listen to this crap while my wife's in there!" he exploded. *"You all can sit out here till hell freezes over, I'm going to get the doctor, now!"*

"Tyrell, you're gonna get us both in trouble, ease up," Kevin interrupted, trying to appeal to his brother's senses.

"I'll lay you out, Kevin, I swear it!" retorted Tyrell.

"Big talk don't make a big man," Kevin shot back.

Spewing forth as many profanities as he could muster, Tyrell stepped in and took a wild swing at his brother. Seeing the hay-maker coming, Kevin quickly leaned sideways, causing Tyrell to tumble headfirst onto the ground.

"That's enough! Pack it up and hit the road, Tyrell, or you'll be spending the night in jail," I said, pulling him up from the lawn. My hand was resting on the nightstick in my belt in case he responded with a swing in my direction.

Kevin stood by me in silence while his brother trotted towards their beat-up station wagon. "This is bullshit...just bullshit," he muttered as he walked away. Moments later, Tyrell spun out of the parking lot, leaving behind a long trail of burnt rubber.

Kevin then decided it was up to him to look after his sister-in-law. The receptionist was still in the process of registering her when we walked back inside. Now feeling in charge of the situation, Kevin briskly approached her and asked in a voice loud enough for everyone to hear, "Peggy, are you still bleeding from your vagina?"

A deep shade of red flowed across Peggy's face as she tried to ignore Kevin.

"Peggy, I said *are you still bleeding from your vagina?*"

The room again echoed with the sound of his voice. Peggy looked up at me with a helpless stare as tears of frustration and embarrassment trickled down her cheeks.

"Kevin, you're going to have to hold it down, or you'll be heading down the highway as well," I said from behind.

He turned and faced me, waving me back with his hands. "Hey, no problem. The last thing I wanna do is go to jail again."

Again? I decided to let his comment slide. As long as he kept quiet, I wasn't going to concern myself with his past.

For the next 20 minutes, Kevin and I sat in relative silence. As time wore on, however, he became increasingly uncomfortable at having to wait. Patience finally exhausted, he insisted I give him permission to go back and see Peggy while she underwent her pelvic exam. I firmly explained to him that the treatment areas were private, and he would have to stay put until the doctor came out. I then suggested we both go outside to get some fresh air. He let out a heavy sigh and shook his head in agreement.

Just as we stepped outdoors, Tyrell pulled back into the parking lot.

"He's probably had time to chill out by now. Wouldn't be surprised if he apologizes for all the trouble," said Kevin.

"He's your brother. You know best."

Kevin nodded his head as he walked over to where Tyrell had parked. The peace lasted only a few seconds. Almost immediately I could hear Tyrell's rising voice lambasting Kevin for not being inside with his wife. Moments later, Tyrell shoved his fists into Kevin's chest, knocking him to the pavement.

I split them up for what I determined would be the final time. Their resentment towards each other was turning into a blood feud. "Tyrell, my patience with you is gone. Take your show somewhere else. If you set foot on this property again, you'll be arrested," I warned.

As Tyrell climbed into the station wagon, his eyes shifted to a catlike stare onto his brother. "This ain't over, Kevin!" he screamed through the window as he roared from the parking lot.

There was something in Tyrell's voice that told me he would be back. My hunch proved right. Thirty minutes later when Tyrell returned, the zone car I'd called in was waiting on him. For a man full of threats, he was unusually silent while handcuffs were snapped around his wrists.

Peggy was discharged from the emergency room shortly afterwards. As she walked down the corridor, she apologized for the disturbance her husband had caused to everyone within listening range. Kevin didn't seem to care; he grabbed her by the arm and quickly guided her towards the exit.

After they were gone, one of the nurses told me Peggy had tearfully broken down in the treatment area after admitting how Tyrell frequently abused her. She further related that the three of them had just arrived in town, stopping overnight in Nashville on their way to New York. They were headed up north to talk a relative out of giving a baby away.

The nurse also said Peggy's most pressing concern wasn't her health, but instead the fear that her husband and brother-in-law would leave her at the hospital and continue on to New York without her.

You would've been better off without them, Peggy.

10

TILL DEATH DO US PART

If you scan a listing of the *Seven Deadly Sins*, you'll notice that jealousy isn't mentioned...at least not directly. Maybe it was recognized as a runner-up in the selection process, but just didn't make the final cut.

Within some marriages, there are those who take it upon themselves to act as the judge, jury and executioner when they feel they've been wronged. A husband or wife does something to hurt their spouse, and in the blink of an eye, a life is ended. It happens all too often.

What's unusual about this scenario is the murderer contacting the police and admitting guilt...especially when we're unaware a murder has even been committed in the first place.

On August 19th, Lyle Crowder quietly walked into the East Station Precinct. Dressed in blue denim from head to heels, he sported an oversized Stetson hat that matched the brown bandanna draped around his neck in a loose triangle. Standing tall in his snake-skinned boots, he looked like the original Marlboro Man.

I didn't give him much thought at first. After all, Nashville is full of wanna-be cowboys. A number of them even drive old Dodge pickup trucks and have a hound dog named Blue riding shotgun with them.

He stopped at the reception area for a minute, taking in the blur of blue uniforms moving around him. After a quick study, he picked his target.

It was the beginning of my shift, and I was standing in front of the sergeant's office reviewing a stack of reports from

119

the previous night. As I flipped through the paperwork, Lyle slowly approached Officer J.R. Whittenburg.

"I just shot my wife and I think she's dead. She's awfully cold," he said in a voice devoid of emotion.

"WHAT?" blurted Whittenburg, full of surprise.

I looked up and saw Whittenburg's eyes narrow to a skeptical stare as they darted between Sergeant Adcox and myself. He was waiting for one of us to crack a smile, thinking we had set him up for a prank.

No one grinned.

The first thing that went through my mind was if this guy *actually did* kill someone, he may still be carrying a gun. I took a couple of quick steps and confronted Lyle. He stood causally in front of J.R.'s desk, offering no resistance while I patted him down. He came up clean.

"You'd better be straight with us on this. Did you really shoot your wife?" I demanded.

"Yeah. I shot her."

"Where is she?"

He lowered his head and sighed heavily, nervously shuffling his heavy boots across the floor.

"Where is she!"

"Back at our place. 4503 Washington Ridge," he whispered.

After telling him to stay with Officer Whittenburg, Sergeant Adcox and I hurried from the station and rushed to the neighborhood where Washington Ridge was located. It was an older section of town, with box-like houses sandwiched between one another on both sides of the street. Given the closeness of the dwellings, it was strange that no one had called in to report a gunshot. Either Lyle's story was a hoax, or the neighbors were afraid to get involved. I hoped it was the former.

The moment we pulled in front of 4503, a puzzled look spread across Sgt. Adcox's face. As I looked up at the residence, his confusion became evident. The house was subdivided into several small apartments, each having a separate entrance.

We didn't have a clue as to which one Lyle lived in.

It was just before 8:00 a.m. and the complex was quiet. We began hammering on doors, rousing the neighbors in an attempt to find Lyle's apartment. The first tenant to respond was a frightened teenager who peered from behind closed curtains.

"Police! We need to know where the Crowders live!" I yelled through the window.

Seeing our uniforms, she quickly pointed down the breezeway towards the last apartment on the left. Sgt. Adcox and I sprinted to the door at the end of the hallway and started pounding. As the seconds ticked by without any response, my stomach began to tighten.

Thinking his wife may be wounded but still alive, we kicked open the door. It swung inward and hit a side wall with a loud crash. Silence followed.

The creaking of the hardwood floor beneath our shoes became the only sounds of life as we moved down the foyer. Turning left, we entered the living room and stopped in our tracks. On the floor in front of the couch was a young lady lying on her back. She was stone cold dead. Next to her body was a .22-caliber rifle.

Jesus, he was telling the truth, I thought, grimacing at the terrified expression frozen into the face of the corpse sprawled on the carpet.

We began searching the apartment, being careful not to disturb any evidence before homicide detectives arrived. With a murder now confirmed, the case would be turned over to them. Still, we felt an inevitable need to piece together the

121

chain of events that precipitated the slaying. We wanted to know what drove Lyle over the edge.

The back bedroom provided the answer. The tiny room was decorated with the gentle grace of a woman; white-laced linen draped the furniture tops, miniature silk flower arrangements dotted the window sills. Hanging above the brass bed was a marriage license issued to Lyle and Melinda Crowder. They had been married exactly two years the previous day. On the nightstand below was a letter Lyle had written to his wife. It was his response to the divorce she had asked for on their second anniversary.

According to the note, Lyle was an aspiring musician who had come to Nashville looking for his "big break". While he worked the local scene in the evenings, he became resentful that his wife went out at night without him. Jealousy took control of his behavior when thoughts of her being with someone else became overwhelming.

Leaving the bedroom, I noticed a medicine bottle on a counter top next to the kitchen. The prescription was made out to Lyle Crowder. The contents read "PROZAC," a drug used to treat depression.

An autopsy later revealed that Melinda had been shot twice in the back and once behind her right ear with the .22-caliber rifle. Lyle Crowder was subsequently charged with criminal homicide and has been in jail since the murder.

And now, several months later, he is attempting to use his dead wife's assets to fund his legal defense against the murder charge.

But not if his mother-in-law has anything to say about it.

Patricia Underwood, the mother of Melinda Crowder, has filed suit to protect her daughter's assets, insisting that justice demands they not be used to defend the alleged murderer. She has requested an immediate hearing on the injunction request and wants a jury trial on her wrongful death claim. Both are still pending.

As Lyle Crowder vegetates in his cell during the hours of nothingness which slowly pass behind bars, certain thoughts of potential defense strategies may cross his mind.

O.J. and Nicole. The Menendez brothers. Tonya Harding and Nancy Kerrigan.

Sorry, Lyle. Without the royalties from a TV movie of the week, I don't think you can afford the high-profile attorney fees. Besides, you already confessed to the murder.

Pleasant dreams.

11

THE WOMAN WITH HAIRY
KNUCKLES

It was late December in 1992. Amidst the snow flurries descending upon Nashville was a flurry of prostitutes featuring holiday specials of a different variety.

Officer Steve Ray and I were assisting an undercover prostitution sting during the latter stages of the holiday season. Our assignment was to follow patrolman Tom Rollins while he attempted to pick-up prostitutes during the operation. Tom was driving an unmarked Honda sedan equipped with a hidden "wire" so that Steve and I, along with another team of officers, would know when a deal had been made. Once the price and services were agreed upon, we would converge on the Honda and make an arrest.

Soon after the operation went into motion, Tom picked up a young male, who was dressed as a female, on lower Dickerson Road. They drove a couple of blocks to a dead-end street where Tom made a deal to receive oral sex for $20.

Once the price was set, Steve and I pulled up behind the Honda and ordered both individuals out of the car. Tom emerged first. He had a sheepish grin on his face, knowing that we would be treating him as a suspect in order not to compromise his cover, and because he was relishing his role as the lead character in our upcoming street production.

The young man then stepped from the car, nonchalantly adjusting his artificial bust in the process.

"I need to see some identification, please," I said, choosing not to call him sir or ma'am just yet.

He stuck a hairy arm into his dress pocket and withdrew a wallet. As he handed me his driver's license, I fought to keep a straight face while glancing at the information on the card.

"Hmmm, this is unusual. Says here your name is Issac Washington. Don't mean to be impolite, but what's a nice girl like you doing with a guy's name?"

"Because I'm a guy, all right? I don't need this shit," he replied in a voice husky enough to pull a dog sled.

Disappointed that none of us were surprised by his admission, he dropped his head and mumbled something about using better make-up in the future.

By this time, Sgt. Fuqua and Officers Jackie Daniels and Gordon Howey had arrived. The cast was now complete. Gathering in a loose circle, we turned our attention towards Tom.

"Did you know you had a guy here?" I scowled at Tom.

"Uh, no, I didn't know what or who-"

"That just ain't natural, son. What's wrong with you?" interrupted Gordon.

Steve moved closer, leaning directly into Tom's face. "I bet you like that kind of stuff!" he huffed.

"You know, I think we've stopped him before, with another guy dressed like a girl," someone else added.

As our accusations continued, Tom's wide-eyed expression left no doubt he felt we were milking too much out of this. But, then again, that just made it more fun to grill him even more.

Meanwhile, Washington had decided on a way out of his predicament and asked to talk with us in private.

"That guy who picked me up ripped me off," he pointed to Tom. "I had twenty bucks from my last, uh, ride... and when I got into the car with this dude, he snatched the money from me."

125

"Do you want to prosecute?" I asked, trying to ignore the wafting smell of his cheap perfume.

"Yeah, if he don't gimme back my twenty," replied Washington.

He apparently figured his "john," in this case, Tom, would simply give him the money to avoid any hassles. He probably felt that even if we wrote him a citation for prostitution, he could go back to work, receiving $20 without having to do anything.

I advised Sgt. Fuqua, the supervisor of the operation, of Washington's claims. Deciding to let the charade continue, Sgt. Fuqua strolled over and confronted Tom.

"I understand you took some money from Mr. Washington."

"If the *judge tells me* to give it back, I will," replied Tom, realizing where this scenario was heading.

We immediately handcuffed Tom and placed him into one of our cars. A marked unit was then summoned to transport Washington to the courthouse so that he could tell his story to the judge.

When we arrived downtown, the twosome were escorted to the committing magistrate. After taking the deposition oath Washington relayed his version of the truth, adamantly accusing Tom of robbing him.

The judge glared at Tom when it was his turn to be sworn in. Casually stretching his shoulders after we uncuffed him, Tom straightened his voice while stroking his chin in thought.

"Your Honor, I picked up Mr. Washington after he offered to perform oral sex for $20. We drove a few blocks and were stopped by the officers standing behind me..."

As Tom continued, he slowly removed the badge case from his rear pocket, opening it slightly so that Washington could see his police identification.

The crowded courtroom started to snicker at this point, anticipating what was about to happen.

"...and I'd like to request a warrant charging Issac Washington with prostitution and filing a false report," Tom finished, gently placing his badge on the table in front of Washington.

Officer Howey stepped up to the judge's bench and waved a cassette in front of Washington. "There's a recorder in the Honda, and this tape has your conversation on it. Would you like me to play it for the whole courtroom to hear?"

Washington began to twitch like a frog during a science experiment. His mouth fell open, speechless at the turn of events.

Although he probably won't make anyone's fashion list, I have to give Washington credit for one thing. He was a good sport about the whole affair, after realizing he'd been set-up.

Gender confusion and prostitution are a strange mix.

12

BLUE LIGHT SPECIALS

"Attention shoppers! For the next 10 minutes, we have a manager's special on aisle 12, where you can save on our famous label Pakistanian oven mitts ..."

The revolving blue light at K-mart was known for its ability to channel customers into narrow aisles like cattle being lead to a daily feeding. It was a simple but effective advertising promotion because it commanded attention.

Many arrests are similar to shopping these blue light specials; some people draw so much attention to their activities, they literally ask to be caught. These crimes are often called "gimmes," because they fall right into your lap.

One afternoon on patrol, I noticed a young blond female parading down a line of cars stopped at a traffic light. Her moneymaking intentions became clear as she drifted from one car to the next, striking up conversations with the drivers. She wasn't attempting to hide her efforts, which was unusual, since most prostitutes will normally direct a car onto a side street or into a parking lot where they won't be so noticeable.

After circling around the block, I pulled over to the side of the street where she was standing and motioned her over to my cruiser. Her hips waved a happy hello with each twisting step she took towards me.

"Hi, officer," she grinned, bending over and placing her barely-clad breasts into the open window. Overwhelmed, I shifted to the right to keep from becoming engulfed in a sea of well-used flesh. Blossoming between her cleavage was a large rose tattoo. A smile was plastered across her thick Barbie Doll make-up while she leaned with one hand propped on the roof of my car, as if this were a casual visit.

"Looks like you're making a lot of friends along the highway. What's going on out here?" I asked.

"Just advertising," she replied with a toothy smile. "I'm tryin' to drum me up some business."

"So what kind of 'business' are you in?"

"My business is pleasure," she seductively winked.

This was too easy, I thought.

"Look, if you don't leave the area, I'm gonna have to arrest you. Consider this a free warning."

"I'll leave if it'll make you happy, but after you're gone, I'll be back out here again."

"Listen closely. Read my lips. I said if you don't get moving, I'm going to arrest you...understand?"

"Of course. Hey, you gotta know the rules before you break 'em, otherwise it's no fun," she laughed.

I shook my head in amazement. It was like a fish asking the fisherman for permission to bite the hook.

"If you want to be arrested, just tell me one thing. Why?" I asked out of curiosity.

"Honest?"

"Honest."

"Well, first of all, I'm not from around here, although I've hooked some in Nashville before. You know, you really have a nice city here. Anyway, I came back cause my mom is in your jail, and I thought that I could visit her for awhile if I got myself arrested."

Being the public servant that I am, I complied with her request, and wished her a happy reunion.

*   *   *   *   *

129

Many of the cases the police department solve aren't always the result of long and intensive investigative work. If the truth be known, a large number of arrests are made because the suspect possessed the IQ of a MoonPie and was careless enough to leave behind a trail which a blind beagle with a cold could follow.

Simply put, if brains were money, some criminals would have to take out a loan for a cup of coffee.

One summer morning I received a call to investigate a rape. A young lady had been sitting in her car waiting for a friend at a local shopping mall when an unknown male jumped into the front seat and forced her to drive to an isolated area. Once there, he repeatedly raped her for over an hour. After the suspect fled, the victim frantically drove to the nearest phone and called the police. Shortly after arriving on location, I transported the young lady to General Hospital, leaving another unit in charge of her car, which was also the crime scene.

On the way to the hospital, she told me the suspect spent several minutes searching for something under the car seats after the rape. Since her pocketbook was in clear view, she had no idea what he could have been looking for, and was too afraid to ask. I relayed this information to the unit still at the scene. Their subsequent search of the vehicle turned up the suspect's wallet, complete with driver's license and photo ID, wedged between a crease in the backseat. The suspect was located and taken into custody shortly afterwards.

A similar circumstance followed several months later. A young lady was driving home one late one afternoon when her car stalled on Charlotte Pike. Unable to coax the vehicle any further, she coasted to the side of the highway. Within a few minutes, a seemingly good samaritan "gentleman" stopped and offered her a ride into town. With some hesitation, the young lady accepted.

Instead of heading towards town, however, the driver took her to a secluded area and raped her. Afterwards, he shoved her from the car and drove off with her clothes. She was left alone, in the middle of nowhere, completely naked.

Drawing upon her strength for vengeance, the victim managed to stumble back into civilization and phoned the police. Although she didn't know the suspect's identity, she told us he stopped at a video store to return some movies after picking her up. We were easily able to identify and apprehend the rapist after checking the video store's records of returns that afternoon.

Apparently, avoiding the $1.50 late charge on his movies was his biggest concern of the day.

Many criminals perform their feats of mischief and mayhem during the evening hours, assuming that the darkness will sufficiently cloak their activities. There are some, however, who are daring enough to strike in broad daylight. Oftentimes these individuals are the ones who act upon impulse, seeing an opportunity they can't resist.

An elderly woman was standing in the check-out line of a Super-X one afternoon, searching through her pocketbook for the money to pay for some merchandise. Behind her lurked a neighborhood thug named Tiny, who tilted the scales at a robust 350 pounds.

Since it was the day social security checks normally arrived, Tiny assumed that when the lady pulled a $50 bill from her purse, she probably had several more of those tucked away inside. After she finished at the check-out, Tiny, seeing easy prey and quick cash flash before his eyes, stepped out of line and followed the fragile lady outside the building.

131

Just as they reached the sidewalk, Tiny snatched her pocketbook and waddled through the crowd milling outside the shopping center. Plowing through the customers with oversized ease, he bumped aside anyone in his path. It was like Moses parting the Red Sea.

He lumbered thirty yards down the firelane and squeezed into a subcompact car, whose plates were registered to his wife. Unfortunately for him, he did this in front of numerous people.

Within an hour we received at least a dozen phone calls from witnesses who provided us with the tag number and Tiny's description. As a result, his reservations were soon confirmed for the luxurious accommodations of the downtown Gray Bar Hotel.

In the end, I'm not sure what bothered Tiny the most...being jailed on theft charges or having to face his angry wife after using her car in the commission of a crime.

There's an old saying in Tennessee that goes *"if you don't like the weather, stick around awhile...it'll change soon enough"*.

During my 14 years on patrol, I've navigated the highways through some of the most inclement conditions, ranging from torrential rain and hail storms to blinding cascades of snow, and even an occasional fog so thick you could spread it with a knife. But it wasn't until the night of May 9th that I had ever encountered a marijuana storm.

I was covering a zone in East Nashville that evening and happened to fall in behind a young man on a motorcycle. Most cyclists normally travel in a relatively straight line down the middle of a lane. However, this individual kept drifting

132

between the left and right lane markings, providing me with enough cause to stop him.

I inched up closer behind him and flipped on my blue lights. Catching the flashing reflections in his rearview mirror, he glanced over his shoulder before popping his cycle into a higher gear and speeding off down the highway.

So, you want to play, I thought, accelerating down the highway after him. I was beginning to shorten the distance between us when he released his right hand from the throttle long enough to reach inside his jacket and pull out a dark object.

My first instinct told me it was a pistol. As I prepared to dodge a spray of gunfire, he withdrew a large baggie and began emptying its contents.

Seconds later, I was engulfed in a marijuana blizzard.

As the grassy substance flew along the pavement, the dampness in the air caused it to stick to my cruiser like flypaper. A green ooze smeared across my windshield the moment I turned on the wipers to regain visibility. To make matters worse, the suspect continued to dump an additional five bags, making my car resemble a large metallic joint as it rolled down the highway after him.

Each time he tossed a baggie, I radioed dispatch the location of the drop. About ten blocks later, several other cruisers joined in on the chase. Feeling the mounting pressure of our increasing numbers, the motorcyclist politely signaled a right turn, then pulled over and stopped. Evidently, he must have thought that once the evidence was gone, all he would get was a speeding ticket.

Wrong.

Several other officers had stopped at the locations where he spilled the dope and gathered up enough of it to provide a good sample. I charged the cyclist with possession for resale and managed to get a conviction based on the evidence. The real kicker is that state law entitled us to seize his motorcycle since it was used to transport the marijuana. The police department gained title to a nice Honda 750 as a result.

No discussion of "gimme" type cases would be complete without paying special tribute to those individuals who rise above the ranks of the typical strong-arm criminal by utilizing their powers of imagination and creativity. These resourceful souls take an innate pride in their illegal efforts, and being cast in the ranks of the average thief is as insulting to them as making obscene references to the heritage of their family members.

For example, I recall the time that a couple of enterprising young men stole an outside mailbox from a post office. Using admirable ingenuity, they subsequently painted it green and stenciled "night deposits" on it. Taking their newly designed box to an area bank, they placed it in front of the drive-thru night deposit box. Their scheme worked...several businesses actually placed their deposits in the redesigned mailbox before someone got suspicious and phoned the police.

Bank robbing just ain't what it used to be.

13

THE TEFLON FACTOR

The typical scenario might involve a police officer sitting at a summer cookout with several of his neighbors.

"I just can't understand it. That pharmaccutical stock I bought last month has already slipped 10 points!" gripes one neighbor.

"At least you still have a job," grumbles another. "The Health Department just slapped my restaurant with some bogus code violations that could shut us down."

The officer half-smiles, acknowledging their problems with a social nod and continues his dinner.

"What 'bout you, Howard? Your day any better?" someone asks the officer.

"Oh, I don't know if better is the word," the officer replies as he casually knifes the rare piece of steak on his plate. "There was the usual assortment of traffic accidents and domestics, but one thing did stick out pretty much from the others. I was called to investigate a stabbing at an abandoned building downtown. I'd only taken a few steps inside when I felt something dripping down on my uniform. I looked up and above me, stuffed in the rafters, was an old wino slashed to pieces. Strange thing was that even though he was dead, he was still smiling. Can you believe it? Smiling. Turned out it was his blood and whatever body fluids he had left that was running down my shoulder. To beat all, I just had my uniform cleaned the day before..."

The conversation around the rest of the table comes to a screeching halt as everyone quietly focuses their attention onto the grilled meat in front of them.

The above "slice of life" depicts the difficulties a cop and those outside their profession have relating to one another at times. It's not purposeful, mind you, but instead the result of not always having common points of reference to share with others. For this reason, cops generally find solace in groups by themselves. They become a subgroup of society, banding together with those having similar backgrounds and experiences. Nothing elitist or antisocial about that, though. After all, it's human nature to seek out those like yourself when socializing, isn't it?

If you consider the subject of police humor, it becomes evident just how pronounced the communication gap is between a cop and the average person. Although varying in extremes among different individuals, a cop's sense of humor can be somewhat crude and distasteful, even borderline gross. It has nothing to do with a lack of respect, but everything to do with keeping your sanity.

When confronted with some of the worst sights a person could possibly imagine, you have to develop a method of bypassing, or "Teflon coating" certain situations. Otherwise, the resulting nightmares will consume your soul like a carnivorous bacteria, making your career in law enforcement relatively short, or else you'll wind up behind padded walls in a mental institution babbling broken sentences no one can understand.

Such was the case with an accident that occurred on I-65 one morning. A person had lost control of his vehicle and slammed into the concrete support barrier of a bridge. Upon impact, the driver was flung out the left window and sent skidding across the highway. When we arrived, his body was lying in the middle of the interstate, his brains scattered across two lanes of traffic. Once units from the traffic division assembled, we began taking the required measurements for our reports. Taping out the scene, we carefully tiptoed around all the gray matter spread on the concrete.

One of the officers watching our efforts was a rookie fresh out of the academy. His contorted facial expressions made it obvious he'd never confronted anything like this before. Upon noticing this, a veteran officer commented in a voice just loud enough for the rookie to hear, "I'm starting to get real hungry guys. Think I'll have me some *scrambled eggs and brains for breakfast.*"

A greenish hue immediately flowed across the rookie's face as he bent over, gagging in effort to relieve himself of last night's dinner.

On a similar note, there was a case some years ago where a couple of officers located a dead body. The deceased was several days expired, judging by the body's decomposition. When one of the officers stooped down to take a closer look, he noticed a small swarm of maggots feasting on the remains.

"Know what these critters remind me of?" he said, turning to his companion.

"What?"

"Onions."

"Onions?" came the confused reply.

"Yeah, reminds me of the little pieces of onions they toss on those fast-food burgers. It's making me hungry. Let's grab a sandwich after we finish up here."

If you're eating while reading this chapter, I apologize.

The above illustrates the "gallows sense of humor" people toss around when they're faced with situations too unsettling to dwell upon. Although some may frown upon this, to a cop it serves as a coping, or better yet, a defense mechanism. It helps form a protective barrier between them and a society which can dish out circumstances few choose to deal with on a daily basis. This veneer of detachment is one way a cops can confront the grotesque events that would otherwise interfere with their ability to carry out assignments in a sane manner. It's not a hardened or callous response, but a method which allows officers to survive in their jobs without going nuts.

A police officer serves as the "catcher's mitt" for whatever ball society throws. The buck stops with them. It's not as if we can turn around and call someone else to handle the gruesome cases. As a result, most cops condition themselves to become more interested in *how something happened,* rather than the tragic consequences. This forces an officer to focus on the situation at hand, determine what's wrong, decide if it's a threat to be dealt with, then find the best solution to the problem.

Although there's a substantial difference in our salaries, we do share one common trait with doctors. Both of us have to place certain feelings aside in order to have a clear perspective on what actions must be taken in particular situations.

Still, there remains one event that even an emotionally detached cop has trouble in handling. It's something considered to be the greatest tragedy of them all, and one which provokes emotions like no other.

Life-threatening injuries to children.

Any cop that has kids can identify with the pain and frustration which rips the soul when dealing with children who have been abused or injured in accidents. I remember working a call once where a parent had accidentally backed a car over their young son playing in the driveway. The child, who later died, was about my son's age. When I got home that evening, I took my boy into my arms and hugged him close while the accident images ran through my thoughts. He was too young to understand what his dad had seen hours before, and the heartache it had left behind.

And that leads to a final thought on this subject. There is a downside in attempting to immunize yourself from certain events. It's that you can't step back from your emotions too far, for you risk losing compassion as well.

And that, God forbid, would be a crime in itself.

14

THE RUNNING MAN

The reflection in the rearview mirror catches you off-guard. Your muscles instinctively tighten as butterflies fill your stomach and goosebumps crawl over your skin like soldier ants on a reconnaissance mission. Slowing to a stop, you quickly turn down the radio and swallow hard, but your suddenly dry throat makes it difficult.

Long seconds pass before there's any movement from behind. Your mind begins racing. *Gotta stay calm...be creative...may be a way out of this...*

Then you hear it. The dreaded voice uttering those words that cause a mental shutdown. Your body slumps forward, signaling the brain defeat is inevitable.

"I need to see your license and registration, please."

Handing out tickets is like patting a stray dog. You never know what kind of response you're going to get. One of the most common is "you should be out catching burglars and rapists instead of hassling me over a simple traffic violation. I pay your salary, you know."

Yes, Mr. Citizen, I realize your taxes help pay my salary. That's why I'm going to make sure you stay alive in order to keep the checks coming.

Consider this...substantially more people die in traffic mishaps than during burglaries and rapes. It's been shown that vigorous traffic law enforcement reduces the number of accidents, according to studies from the Northwestern Traffic Institute, THE authority on accident statistics. Thus, "work radar, not wrecks" is a philosophy adopted by many departments.

In order to issue a ticket, you have to assume the traffic violator is going to stop and grudgingly accept it. There are, however, those who subscribe to the philosophy "only the meek get pinched, the bold speed away."

Metro's department policy on high-speed pursuits has changed dramatically since I joined the force. The Sheriff Buford T. Justice "hot pursuit" method of apprehending suspects made famous in *Smokey and the Bandit* are a thing of the past. Increased attention to individual rights, insurance liabilities and the inherent risks involved with running a cruiser at full bore have taken care of that.

Up until the late 1970's, however, high-speed chases were still in vogue. Back then, if someone sped off after we tried to stop them for a minor traffic infraction, we would chase them all the way to Kentucky, burying our speedometers on the high side in the process.

Painfully etched into my memory is the first pursuit I was ever involved in. As a rookie fresh out of the academy, I was riding with Officer Walter Keeler one evening while he patrolled some projects in the downtown area. Several groups of teenagers stared and nodded their heads as we approached in our cruiser, then flipped us "the bird" the moment we passed by, unaware that rearview mirrors actually do work.

"Don't take it personally. It's not you they're trashing, it's the uniform. Always remember that. Besides, it's better to be shot by the bird than shot by a gun," Walter laughed.

I couldn't argue with his logic. He had ten-plus years on patrol. I had maybe ten days at best.

While we circled the neighborhood, we picked up a call from another station concerning a traffic violation pursuit heading our way. When the suspect's car left the interstate and turned toward the projects, Walter roared down Gallatin Road

141

with the accelerator mashed to the floor in order to intercept the vehicle. I froze with the stiffness of a corpse when I glanced over and saw the speedometer accelerating at warp speed. The cars we soared past became a blur of Disney-like colors as I squeezed my safety belt with a death grip, praying to the powers above, and any others that might have been listening, that we wouldn't hit anything.

Just as we closed in on the suspect's car, he spun out of control around a sharp corner and slammed into a utility pole. We came to a sliding stop behind the wreckage in time to see the suspect bolt upright in his seat. The fear which had gripped my senses earlier quickly vanished. It was immediately replaced with fury.

I jumped from our cruiser and hit the ground at full sprint. Within an instant, I was bashing on the suspect's car windows, swinging my entire body weight behind each bare-handed blow as if taking shots at a punching bag. The suspect gawked at me while the car shook from the repeated poundings. His mouth was dropped open and his eyes filled with fear...the same fear I had moments earlier.

Realizing my determination to get to him, and that the thin glass wasn't going to stop me much longer, the suspect slid away from the driver's window to the far side of the car. Moments later, two other officers arrived and managed to pull him out of the passenger compartment. I was left standing alone and out of breath, bruised hands dangling painfully at my sides. It made no sense. The suspect had totaled his car, jeopardized his life, our lives and compromised the safety of those on the street during his attempt to elude us...and it was all over a minor traffic violation.

When an officer engages in a pursuit, there is always the possibility someone will be injured in the process. It's a risk that sometimes can't be avoided, and, as a result, there have been several fatalities in Davidson County which have directly or indirectly been linked to chases.

One night in Madison, Ed Stanfield was routinely patrolling Myatt Drive, a straight four-lane road that was a popular spot for kids to gather, a place where they could flex their fuel-injected muscles on Friday nights.

While on this stretch of highway, Ed spotted a couple of teenagers drag-racing. Upon seeing his cruiser, both cars abruptly sped off, one going straight down Myatt Drive and the other turning down a nearby side street. Ed began his pursuit after the vehicle which had turned, feeling it would be easier to catch.

The suspect veered onto another road as Ed continued to follow. Unfortunately, the car's occupants weren't familiar with this particular street, which contained a sharp dog-legged turn that ran alongside a high riverbank. The car's brakelights never flickered as it entered the winding passageway. Seconds later, the vehicle tore through a guardrail and sailed high above the tree tops before dropping into the river. The two juveniles inside drowned.

Courts have recently determined that pursuits are unconstitutional in a number of situations. Their decisions are based upon the fourth amendment which prohibits unreasonable search and seizures. Using a form of deadly force, such as a high speed pursuit to arrest a person is deemed unreasonable in misdemeanor situations. An example of this revolves around a case decided in Tullahoma, Tennessee.

One afternoon, officers observed two teenagers turning doughnuts in a car at a crowded shopping center. When the officers tried to stop them, the juveniles raced from the center and onto the connecting highway. Emergency lights activated, they chased the vehicle at high speeds, but were unable to match its acceleration. The teenagers' car quickly moved out of sight. After advising their supervisor of the situation, they

143

were instructed to reduce speed, but to proceed with blue lights flashing as they attempted to locate the vehicle.

Minutes later, the officers found the suspects' car. It was wrapped around a large oak tree several miles down the highway. The passenger, embedded in the twisted wreckage, was dead on arrival. His parents subsequently sued the police department and collected a sizable judgment.

Not all pursuits are the result of high-speed chases...some actually end before they have a chance to begin.

Confused? Let's just say that sometimes those we are hired to serve and protect have a tendency to serve up their own form of protectionism from time to time.

Some years back I received a 10-53 (armed robbery in progress) call occurring at a grocery store at the far end of the county. The store straddled a crossroads in a sparsely populated rural area, and even though I was over 15 miles from the scene, I was the closest unit in the vicinity. After being told that shots had been fired, I hit my blue lights and siren and hurdled down the highway in an attempt to arrive as soon as possible.

The action was over by the time I pulled up to the grocery store, but its aftermath remained. Directly across the highway was a silver Camaro with its front end resting on top of a guard rail. The driver was spewing forth blood from a large head wound and was unconscious. I rendered what first-aid I could and then radioed dispatch to request Med-Com assistance.

Watching the flurry of activity from the parking lot across the street was a lone figure dressed in overalls. He stood in the evening shadows, hands buried in his pockets. As

144

I walked towards him, his rugged, deeply lined faced turned pale.

"Guess I'm in trouble, huh?" he said, slowly reaching into his back pocket and withdrawing a pouch of tobacco. His hands trembled as he raked the stems between his fingers.

"Quit drinking 20 years ago, so this is what I use to calm the nerves," he whispered while placing a wad between his cheeks. "The name's Miller. I own the business next door."

He took a deep breath between his chew, then aired a stream of tobacco juice with stealth precision onto a curb six feet away. "I suppose you want to know what happened," he uttered in a hoarse voice. Looking towards the Camaro, he began to relate the events which took place minutes earlier.

Mr. Miller had been standing at the gas pumps in front of the grocery store when two men wearing ski masks ran out of the business. Assuming they had just robbed the grocery, he grabbed a .357 magnum from his car as the pair jumped into their vehicle. Seeing the weapon in Miller's hand, one of the suspects turned and fired wildly in his direction.

After the round ricocheted off the pavement behind him, Miller returned fire at the fleeing car. He squeezed off a single shot, sending a lone bullet through the rear window. It shattered the glass and struck the driver dead-center in the back of the head. He died shortly after Med-Com arrived.

The second suspect jumped from the car and ran into the nearby woods after his buddy was hit. Helping his partner was the last thing on his mind; he was more concerned with saving his own butt. I wound up calling in a canine officer and searched the area for several hours. Although we were unable to locate him, he was apprehended not long afterwards.

That afternoon Mr. Miller single-handedly confronted two individuals who could've turned him into a toe-tagged stiff at the morgue for interfering with their robbery. What the suspects hadn't bargained for, however, was running into

145

someone who refused to stand in the background and idly watch their rampage. Someone who, in all regards, was fed up with criminals preying on society.

It bears mentioning that Mr. Miller wasn't charged on any counts for taking the life of the would-be robber. In the court records, it was simply noted he aided officers in a felony apprehension.

Kill a man for his money, they call you a murderer. Kill a man because he's trying to steal someone else's money, they call you a hero.

Go figure.

The next time you're out driving at night and see another car without headlights on, remember this story. It might save a life.

It was just past midnight on a Saturday, and I was traveling down a quiet stretch of highway shortly after leaving roll-call. It was a peaceful evening, the clear weather allowing a half-moon to cast its dim light across the star-packed sky. The radio was silent, the traffic was light. Relaxation.

My attention drifted onto the opposite lane as I tilted a soft-drink upwards and peered over its rim. A green Cadillac with its headlights off was fast approaching. Usually this isn't a big deal; lots of people momentarily forget to turn on their headlights when starting out into the night. Oncoming drivers will normally blink their lights as a reminder, and then everything is taken care of. Still, it was a late weekend night, and there would be partied-out souls behind too many wheels.

The car disappeared over a slight rise in the road behind me as I turned my cruiser around and headed back in the opposite direction to check on the driver. Less than a minute later,

I rolled across the rise and confronted a devastating two-vehicle accident.

"Unit 12, 10-46 at 1447 Dickerson Road, 10-47 (ambulance) *needed immediately!"* I shouted into the radio before slinging the mike into the floorboard.

As I ran towards the demolished wreckage, the angle of the cars gave me the impression that the second vehicle, an old Plymouth, had been approaching the Cadillac from the opposite direction. The driver of the Plymouth apparently didn't see the car with its lights off, and attempted to turn left in front of the Cadillac. A massive head-on collision resulted.

The woman driving the Cadillac was leaning over the crushed dashboard, spitting out teeth, when I knelt next to the twisted remains of her car. A deep gash across her forehead bore the same curvature as the steering wheel. Though she was banged up, bruised and bloody, her injuries weren't life-threatening.

The driver of the Plymouth suffered multiple injuries as well, but like the woman in the Cadillac, none of them was critical. I then shifted my attention to the passenger in the Cadillac. She was unconscious; her labored breathing came in spasmodic jerks as she instinctively fought for oxygen. Her left foot was twisted at an odd angle beneath her where a pool of blood was spreading across the floorboard. Given the rate and amount of blood loss, I knew she was in serious trouble.

I reached over to check her pulse, gently sweeping aside the long brown hair tangled across her face. Her soft cheeks were tanned and smooth, with a few light freckles sprinkled around her nose. She was on the brink of becoming a beautiful young woman at 17 or 18, an age where she undoubtedly enjoyed the admiration of countless young bucks vying for her attention.

Not knowing what kind of internal injuries she may have had, I stayed in the car with her until Med-Com arrived a few

147

minutes later. As the paramedics lifted her from the vehicle, I looked down at her ankle. Her left foot was almost completely sheered off, and was dangling from her shin by a thin piece of skin.

Before the paramedics could get her into the ambulance, she went into cardiac arrest. As they furiously began CPR on her, for a moment, the briefest of seconds, her eyes cracked open and met mine. I don't know if there was enough life left in her to comprehend what she saw. A man...a stranger...a cop. Whatever image she may have seen, it was to be her last.

It's hard to say why I remember this accident more so than some others. Maybe it's because the simple flick of a headlight switch could have prevented it. Maybe it's because if I had encountered the Cadillac further up the highway, none of this would have happened. Or maybe, it was the look I saw in the young girl's eyes the moment before she died.

Maybe, just maybe.

Two hours later I'm issuing a speeding ticket to some teenagers going too fast down the same stretch of highway. They don't understand the firmness in my voice and the frown on my face while I hand them the citation. I don't try to explain it to them. They wouldn't understand.

As I walk back to my cruiser, one of the occupants remarks that I should be doing something more important than chasing cars...

15

YES, VIRGINIA, THERE IS A BOOGEYMAN

The winter sun was beginning to heat up the car's interior as I settled into the seat next to my partner, Danny Baxter.

The dark blue uniform which had dutifully absorbed the punches, kicks and head-butts directed at me throughout the years had recently given way to plainclothes. After 12 years on patrol, I was now working as a burglary investigator at East Station.

It had been a slow week, so Danny and I decided to bail out of the office for awhile and answer some calls with the patrol officers on the chance we might be able to stir up some business for ourselves. After the routine stop for a sausage biscuit, we began circling our sector looking for a crime to solve.

Before we had a chance to find one, one found us.

"Car 24, 10-71P (burglary in process) *at 814 Scenic Drive. Complainant advises that she returned home and was badly beaten by several males who were inside her residence,"* came the call over the radio as we made our second sweep of the sector. Unit 24 was assigned to Officer Jerry Dobbins, and once he acknowledged the call, I advised the dispatcher we would respond as back-up.

The neighborhood around Scenic Drive was filled with older frame houses, with newer duplexes occupying every available lot between the antique structures. Generally a quiet neighborhood, this area seldom presented any problems, other than the few domestic calls which occur without regard to the economic status of an area.

We pulled onto the scene moments after Jerry, and were immediately confronted with a frantic 15-year-old on the sidewalk in front of the residence. Her face was bruised and swollen, leaving us no doubt she had been on the wrong side of an altercation. She identified herself as Megan Schlister, and told us she had just returned home after spending the night with a girlfriend. She went on to explain that after entering her house, she was attacked by several males hiding inside.

Danny requested Med-Com to the scene, and remained with Megan while Jerry and I conducted a fruitless search for any suspects remaining inside. The only unusual thing we found was a bedroom door which had been hit with enough force to completely rip it from the surrounding hardwood frame. No other evidence of a struggle was apparent within the small, neatly kept residence. Oddly enough, there were no signs of a forced entry into the home itself, but instead a single, damaged door outside the bedroom.

Once Med-Com and Megan's mother arrived at the house, Danny joined us in the hallway. We were discussing the incident when one of the paramedics interrupted our conversation.

"You guy's seen the writing on this girl's back?"

We turned around, puzzled at his remark, and saw him shaking his head in disbelief.

"Beats anything I've ever seen," he continued, motioning towards the door.

We followed him outside and into the yard where Megan was standing. She was turned away from us, her sweatshirt rolled up to her shoulders. On her back were bite marks, along with the words, 'I am a whore and a slut' written in bright red lipstick.

150

A combination of shock and anger was stretched across the face of Megan's mother. "Send your Med-whatever back. I'll take her to the doctor myself...right now," Mrs. Schlister choked.

"Let me make a suggestion," I said. "Since Megan doesn't seem to need immediate medical attention, why don't we all go inside and sort this situation out."

She hesitated a moment before replying, struggling to regain her composure. Tears welled up in her eyes as she looked at her daughter, who stood by in silence, head hung in shame. Mrs. Schlister then nodded towards the house, and the five of us went back inside.

Once seated in the living room, we explained to Megan that the markings on her back and the lack of any visible means of forced entry into the home led us to believe there was more to her story than she had admitted. She slowly withdrew to a corner of the couch, curling into a near-fetal position without replying.

"Megan, it's all right to be scared. We understand. Believe me, we're here to help you, but we need to know the full story before we can do anything," I said.

Unable to make eye contact, Megan locked her gaze onto the hardwood floor beneath her as she nervously fumbled with the key chain in her hands. Speaking in low whisper, she tearfully revealed a different version of what happened.

She told us that the day before a friend of hers, Ellen Cowler, called and invited her over to spend the night. She agreed and was picked up later in the evening by Ellen and a couple of boys she knew only as Calvin and "Skeeter", both about 18 or 19 years old.

They went to an upstairs apartment situated over a house in the lower end of East Nashville, where some guy and his girlfriend Deanna lived. Deanna was alone for the weekend and had invited some people over for a party. Megan wasn't sure of the exact address, but thought the apartment was some-where near Eleventh or Fifteenth Street.

Sweeping the moisture from her eyes, Megan continued, explaining that after they'd been at the apartment for a couple of hours, Calvin and Ellen went to a nearby market to buy something to drink. They soon returned with another girl, a 14-year-old named Beverly. The party continued, and every-one seemed to be getting along fine. As midnight approached, the alcohol inventory bottomed out, prompting the other girls to leave in search of beer before the stores closed. Megan was left alone with Calvin and "Skeeter" in the meantime.

"When they came back an hour later, Beverly started looking at me like, weird, you know. She jumped in my face and yelled I was giving her a "funky" look. I told her I didn't know what she was talking about, but she wouldn't listen. We got into a fight, and she beat the crap out of me," she said, rub-bing her hands across the bruises on her face.

Megan went on to explain that after the fight, everyone became concerned about the damage Beverly's blows left on her face. Afraid to let her go home in such a battered condi-tion, she told us the group made her stay at the apartment until morning. By then, they reasoned, the swelling would subside and make her injuries less noticeable.

When morning arrived, she was escorted home by the other teenagers. Once inside the house, the girls restrained her on the couch while Calvin and "Skeeter" broke through the door leading to her father's bedroom. They emerged several minutes later with two of his handguns.

"I was so scared...I didn't know what to do. After what they'd done to me, I was afraid they'd kill me," Megan softly cried as she clutched a sofa cushion tightly to her chest. "I told them I wouldn't tell no one, nobody at all. They must've believed me, cause they all left after that."

Satisfied the truth had been told, Mrs. Schlister stood up and took her daughter by the hand. "We're going to the doctor," she said, guiding Megan towards the door. Before they walked out, Mrs. Schlister abruptly stopped and turned back towards us.

"I want to prosecute all of them! You hear me? Every last one of them! Those beasts will pay for this!" she yelled, anger ripping through her clinched teeth.

"We're going to do everything we can, Mrs. Schlister. Make sure you have pictures taken of Megan's injuries, as well as the markings on her back for evid-" My words were cut off by the door slamming behind them.

Although Mrs. Schlister was convinced her daughter had given us a truthful account of the incident, Danny and I still had our doubts. We left the scene and drove to the general vicinity where Megan described the assault took place. In order to confirm her story, we needed to locate the apartment where the attack occurred, as well as determine the identity of the guys involved. We circled the area several times, but were unable to match Megan's vague description of the building to anything we saw. We also spoke with several officers who worked in nearby zones, but no one seemed to know who Calvin or "Skeeter" were. Exhausting our leads, we headed back towards the station with the promise that should anyone come across any information relating to our case, they would contact us.

The shift rotation was just beginning as Danny and I wandered back into our office. "It's past time to call it a day, partner," Danny remarked, looking at his watch.

I shoved aside the pile of paperwork heaped on my desk and reached for the phone. Tearing off an assortment of post-it notes that littered the receiver during our absence, I began dialing.

"Giving Ellen Cowler one last try?"

153

I nodded as the phone started ringing. We had tried contacting her several times earlier without success. Our hope was that Ellen could fill in some of the gaps we felt were missing from Megan's story, and shed some light on the identities of Calvin and "Skeeter" as well.

After about a dozen rings the phone was finally answered by Ellen's mother. She told me Ellen hadn't been home since yesterday, and she didn't have any idea where her daughter had been the last 24 hours. The disappointment in her voice equaled my own.

"Another dead-end," I muttered, hanging up the phone.

The feeling of overlooking something was gnawing at my gut. The few pieces of information needed to confirm Megan's story dangled just beyond our grasp. Even though we knew Megan had been assaulted, something about the whole situation still didn't make sense.

"Tomorrow. Fresh start. There's too many people involved in this case for us not to find out the truth," Danny remarked, sensing the frustration in my voice.

"Yeah, tomorrow," I echoed, trying to convince myself while reaching for my jacket.

"Maybe tomorrow."

By 7:30 the next morning, Danny and I were back at our desks reviewing the notes relating to Megan's case. Since nothing else had fallen into place, it was time to start back at the beginning. I phoned Mrs. Schlister and asked her to bring Megan down to the station for another interview. We were banking on the assumption that Megan would be calmer than the day before, and be able to provide a more detailed account of the people and events involved in her assault. Megan and her mother arrived within an hour. As we sat down to start covering her story piece by piece, a voice floated over one of the office partitions.

"Hey, Baxter. Line two's been holding for you."

"Tell 'em I call back in a few minutes," Danny responded.

"Think you better take this one. It's an officer from the Central Sector. Says he may have something for you on yesterday's assault."

Mrs. Schlister's eyes lit up as Danny grabbed the phone. Megan's face remained expressionless. About a minute later, Danny hung up and reached across the desk for his car keys.

"One of the officers we talked to yesterday just arrested an armed teenager in the neighborhood where Megan said she was attacked. It may or may not relate to our case, but I'm going to check it out," he said.

As Danny walked out of the room, Mrs. Schlister turned towards me. "I've got something to show you. A guy I've never seen before came by where I work this morning and gave me this," her voice trailed off as she reached into her purse and withdrew one of the two pistols taken in the burglary.

"The guy asked if I had a daughter named Megan," she continued, "and when I said yes, he handed me the gun in a plastic bag. He said his nephew gave it to him the night before and told him it was a gift from Megan. He wouldn't tell me anything else, except that he didn't want to get involved. Then he walked off."

While I was discussing this unusual visit with the Schlisters, Danny was uncovering some information which convinced him Megan had been raped during the assault. He phoned the station to tell me he had contacted Sexual Abuse Detective Suzanne Stephens, who would be meeting with us shortly.

Danny walked into the station about 30 minutes later. With him were three of the suspects in the case. As he escorted them down the hallway, the scowl on his face

155

confirmed whatever new evidence he had discovered, it wasn't good. I took Megan back to our office and waited for Danny to join us. He strolled in several minutes later, shutting the door behind him.

"Megan," he quietly said, "we've taken Calvin into custody for possession of the handgun stolen from your house. In the process, he's given us a different description of what happened the night you were assaulted. From his statements, I was able to locate two of the other individuals involved."

Danny shifted uncomfortably on his feet as he looked directly at Megan. "I know how difficult this is going to be for you, Megan, but we need to verify his story."

She leaned forward in her chair, eyes glistening with moisture. Her face turned pale while she struggled to find the words to answer Danny.

"I was raped, but that's not all," she blurted, burying her head into her hands. *"That's not all there was to it!"*

Danny and I stood by in silence, waiting for her tears to subside. We then briefly confirmed the basic events of Calvin's story with her. Deciding not to go any further, we waited for Detective Stephens to arrive so Megan would have to go through the complete story just once.

Once was enough. As Megan gave Detective Stephens a detailed account of the incident, both Danny and I were overwhelmed with the viciousness of her attackers. All the events which occurred prior to the time that she, Calvin and "Skeeter" were left alone in the apartment remained the same. The reality from that point on changed from her original version.

After learning the acts of cruelty and abuse she had been subjected to, I finally understood her hesitancy in acknowledging them.

Once the three of them were alone, Calvin and "Skeeter" forced Megan to have sex with them. They later argued it was consensual, but that didn't matter. A 15-year-old cannot legally give consent to have intercourse.

When everyone else returned, they caught the trio in the act. Beverly, who liked Calvin, became upset when she discovered him having sex with Megan. Temper snapping, she lunged at Megan, and a fight ensued. Moments later, both Deanna and Ellen jumped in and sided with Beverly. Megan didn't have a chance against the three of them.

After being beaten into submission, Megan was given a guided tour of Hell over the next several hours. She was forced to perform oral sex on a dog which Deanna smothered onto her face, then was commanded to ride the other girls around on her back like a horse after being stripped naked. As the group further degraded her with insults and taunts, she was ordered to shave her pubic hair, and then choke down a drink containing a mixture of the other girl's urine. As a final act of humiliation, Megan was forced to spoon up the dog feces on the floor and swallow it.

Surprisingly, after Detective Stephens interviewed Deanna, she didn't deny her part in the ordeal. Deanna was transported to booking and subsequently charged with aggravated rape.

While Danny and Detective Stephens interviewed the other suspects in the case, I drove to the address where the attack took place. I was met there by one of our identification officers, Tim Mason, who offered assistance with processing the crime scene.

We entered the apartment and were confronted by two large dogs in the hallway. Their attention towards us was brief; their main concern was chasing several cats scrambling throughout the cramped, two-bedroom quarters. As the dogs closed in on their prey, the cats leaped into the living room closet and buried themselves deeply into the mounds of trash piled high inside.

The living room was bare, with the exception of a cushionless worn-out sofa and a small black-and-white television on a bookcase. As we made our way towards the kitchen, the stench of rotting food flooded the air. The room was filthy. Decaying table scraps littered the countertops and the stained walls were crawling with a platoon of roaches.

The bedroom next to the kitchen was empty except for some blankets and clothes stuffed into the corner. In the other, several piles of dog feces were scattered across the wooden floor. Within one was a spoon. Next to it was coarse puddle of vomit. Tim winced as he photographed the evidence in silence.

In all the years I've answered calls in people's homes, I can't remember one with nastier conditions. It was unfit for human, even animal habitation.

While I drove back to the station, the sight of the spoon laying in the excrement was frozen in my mind. The haunting images of what Megan had to endure became embedded in my thoughts and sickened me. I silently vowed to make this case as airtight as possible and push for a conviction with the same lack of compassion shown to Megan by her abusers.

An hour later, Danny and I re-interviewed Calvin. While we videotaped his statement, he provided his version of the incident. He claimed that he was an observer only and couldn't get "aroused" enough to have sex with Megan. He further insisted that he warned the others they "shouldn't be subjecting Megan to such treatment." Based on his statement, Calvin was charged with both aggravated rape and aggravated burglary. He also revealed who "Skeeter" was, and "Skeeter" surrendered himself to us the next day, to be similarly charged.

Beverly and Ellen were also charged for their participation. At least one of them is still undergoing psychiatric treatment. None of the individuals involved requested a trial. They knew better than to have a jury hear the case.

I have a daughter who is a few years younger than Megan. For sometime after, whenever I looked into her trusting eyes, I was reminded of the horrors Megan had been subjected to. In the span of one evening, her carefree teenage years had been lost forever. Painfully etched in their place would be the memories of a night she may never be able to put behind her.

Yes, Virginia, there is a boogyman...and he has friends.

16

"THAT'S ME, THE LOUSY COP"

"Well, Mr. Citizen, I guess you have me figured out. I seem to fit neatly into the category you have placed me into. I'm stereotyped, characterized, standardized, classified, grouped and always typical. I'm the lousy cop!

Unfortunately, the reverse isn't true. I can never figure you out. From birth you teach your children that I am the bogeyman, and then you're shocked when they identify me with my traditional enemy, the criminal. You accuse me of coddling juveniles, until I catch your kid doing something. You may take a hour for lunch and several coffee breaks each day, but point me out as a loafer if you see me having just one cup. You pride yourself on your polished manners, but think nothing of interrupting my noon meals with your troubles. You raise hell about the guy who cut you off in traffic, but let me catch you doing the same thing and I'm picking on you. You know all the traffic laws, but never got one single ticket you deserved. You shout "foul" if you observe me driving fast, enroute to an emergency call, but literally raise hell if I take more than ten seconds responding to your call.

You call it "part of my job" if someone strikes me, but it's "police brutality" if I strike back. You wouldn't think of telling your dentist how to pull a badly decayed tooth, or your doctor how to take out your appendix, but you are always willing to give me a few pointers on law enforcement. You talk to me in a manner and use language that would assure a bloody nose from anyone else, but you expect me to stand there and take it all without batting an eye. You cry "something has to be done about all this crime," but you can't be bothered with "getting involved."

You've got no use for me at all, but, of course, it's O.K. if I change a tire for your wife, or deliver your baby in the back-seat of my patrol car on the way to the hospital, or save your son's life with mouth-to-mouth resuscitation, or work many hours overtime to find your lost child.

So, Mr. Citizen, you stand there on your soapbox and rant about the way I do my job, calling me every name in the book, but never stop a minute to think that your property, your family, or maybe your life might depend on one thing...me, or one of my buddies."

"THAT'S ME, THE LOUSY COP"

This article was written by Troopers Mitchell and Brown (now staff sergeant Larry Brown, 272nd Military Police Company, Manneheim, Germany), of the Virginia State Police. Two months after it was published, Trooper Mitchell was killed in an automobile crash while enroute to an accident at a West Virginia coal mine. His patrol car was struck by a drunk driver.

Not too long ago, as time goes, a new form of music was born.

It was laced with a strange, yet compelling rhythm that sparked an unusual, even riotous excitement from the younger generation who were mystically drawn to it with wild abandonment. The words put to this music sometimes rhymed without reason. They spoke of free love, protest...of individual rights.

The elders of society scorned its emergence, partly because they couldn't understand the unusual words or relate to its gyrating rhythm. They would preach to whomever would listen that this music threatened to rip apart the very fabric of a moral society. The songs were subsequently labeled as ghoulish, satanic, even deranged. And, if nothing else, just a passing fad.

But this fad did not pass. When rock-and-roll was born, it was destined to live a long and prosperous life.

Even accepted, after hesitation, by some of its detractors.

During the last 35 years, rock-and-roll has flourished, and has borne offspring too numerous to mention. We can now feast upon a musical smorgasborg--there's a sound for everyone.

And now there's something called rap.

Being a resident of Nashville, I have to admit that I'm a bit partial to country music. And although I don't normally scan the radio dial searching for a rap station, I do know enough about this type of music to realize it generally addresses the same subjects as rock--social reform, love, human rights, and so on. That's all well and good.

Unfortunately, however, some rap music has crossed the line of good taste and has spoken of something entirely different.

Killing cops.

One of these "songs" I refer to is by the rap group *Ice-T*. The name of their 1993 hit was "Cop Killer", and its popularity placed the record high upon Billboard's Top 100 most requested songs during that year.

If you've never heard this "song", the following lyrics may surprise, even offend you. Quite frankly, I hope they do both.

"I got my black shirt on,
I got my black gloves on,
I got my ski mask on,
This shit been too long.
I got my 12-gauge sawed off,
I got my headlights turned off,
I'm about to bust some shots off.
(Chorus)
Cop killer, it's better you than me,
Cop killer, fuck police brutality.
Cop killer, I know your family's grievin'
Fuck 'em!
Cop killer, but tonight we get even,
I got my brain on hype,
Tonight will be your night,
I got this long ass knife,
And your neck looks just right.
My adrenaline's pumpin'
I got my stereo bumpin'
I'm about to kill me somethin'
A pig stopped me for nuthin'
(Chorus)
Die, die, die, pig, die!
Fuck the police!"

I find it hard to believe that Warner Bros. Records (yes, part of the same organization which brings us *Bugs Bunny, Batman* and *Time* magazine) would actually market a record containing these lyrics. Even more incredible is that people would actually *support* this type of crap by purchasing it.

I wonder how the executives in Warner Bros. ivory tower would feel if a group produced a record encouraging their deaths.

Was this song conceived as an attempt to make a social statement about the abuse some of the underclass suffers from those in power?

Maybe.

Will it intensify the hostile feelings already present in these individuals and lead them to riot against authority?

Probably not.

Most people are smarter than that. But, then again, there will always be some individuals whose minds are so twisted and impressionable, that they will latch onto lyrics such as those in "Cop Killer" and act upon them like soldiers being lead into battle.

July 1992. While on patrol, two Las Vegas police officers were ambushed and shot by four juveniles who later boasted the song "Cop Killer" gave them the idea, the motivation on how to "get even by killing cops." While in custody, the four chanted the song's lyrics over and over.

Yes, I'll admit there are those in our profession who occasionally step beyond the boundaries of using reasonable force to make an arrest. But for every cop who does that, there are hundreds, literally thousands, who wind up getting injured themselves because they used *too little restraint* in apprehending a suspect.

The song "Cop Killer" is laced with hatred and vile prejudice throughout its deplorable lyrics. Still, the record posted strong sales, and I can't understand why.

Perhaps it's time the police force came out with their own rap song personifying the frustration *they feel* in dealing with criminals on a daily basis.

With that in mind, I submit the following idea:

"Yo, Mr. Criminal, now that you're behind bars,
For killing, maiming and selling drugs while stealin' cars.

Rememberin' all the havoc you wrecked on society,
I hope you'll just sit in your cell and think quietly.
(Chorus)
And just when I think I put a dent in your crimes,
When all those you abused are singin' you're doin' time.
I look around and you're back on the street,
Walking cockedly yellin' you can't be beat."

How about it, Warner Bros.? Want to give our side some equal time?

Class-labeling all cops *for any particular action* makes as much sense as assuming all mechanics will pad your bill at the service station. It's as absurd as saying that all Italians are card-carrying members of the Mafia, or all businessmen and politicians are crooks, based on the few who elected to defraud the public for their own personal gain.

Guys, wake up. It just doesn't work that way.

Today's police officer is constantly being scrutinized, analyzed and theorized under a public microscope which has no limitations, a microscope which often neglects to focus on a key issue of law enforcement. If you want the law to respect you, then you have to respect the law.

And when it's all been said and done, debated and rehashed, one fact still persists...cops are the last and final line between law and lawlessness, the one separating factor between sanity and anarchy.

And if not us, *then who?*

The judges, perhaps even the lawyers?

I don't think so. It's the everyday, ordinary cops who have to roll up their sleeves and tackle the problems of society that others choose to ignore or pretend don't exist.

It's "Officer Friendly" who has to face off against the deviants that would give anything to molest your son or

165

daughter, who has to confront the burglar who wants nothing more than to steal, and subsequently pawn, your most valued possessions for cocaine money.

It's "Joe Cop" that works the midnight to eight shift, who seldom sees his wife or kids, so you can pause at a stop light at the crack of dawn without fearing for your life. It's the undercover officers who risk their lives shutting down crack houses so our streets don't become a flea market for drug vendors.

It's all the people who give their hearts and souls, and sometimes even their lives, in order to try and make the playing field a little more equal.

And that brings us back to the same question which began this book: *What's it like to be a police officer?*

At this point, I hope you'll be able to answer that on your own.

Rest easy, people, but keep one eye open. We can't do it all by ourselves.

We've got to have your help.

ADDENDUM

As this book was going to press, tragedy again struck the Metro Nashville Police Department.

Officer Paul Scurry was a policeman's policeman. More importantly, he was a friend of mine. After I graduated from the police academy, I rode with Paul for several months. We covered the Madison area on the midnight shift, back when the zone was nicknamed "Maytag Land," after the famed repairman who had nothing to do.

Since this was a quiet area, Paul and I would occasionally stop by his apartment to remedy a case of the midnight munchies. As I got to know the person behind the shield, I learned that Paul was an avid hunter, had a fondness for Willie Nelson music, and even became acquainted with his young daughter when she came to visit her father. Paul also enjoyed photographing old barns, and more than one sunrise caught us on the side of the road, Paul's camera on a tripod, taking pictures of a newfound structure while the early morning light slowly enveloped the landscape.

On May 17, 1996, my friend Paul became another victim consumed by the senseless violence which threatens to bring our country to its knees.

It was midmorning on the 17th when I walked into the East Station Precient. I sat down at my desk for a few minutes to catch up on the paperwork which I continually run behind on. As I shuffled one pile to another, I listened to the portable radio on my desk in order to monitor the radio traffic. Before long, a detective requested a patrol car to assist in serving a warrant. I didn't think much of it, as it's usually just a routine

167

event which occurs several times a day. A minute or two later someone yelled, *"Code 5000! Officer shot!"*

I jumped from the desk and ran out to my car, making a quick trip to the River Retreat Apartments on Cheyenne Boulevard in Madison. Numerous cars were already on the scene, with more screeching to a halt every second. I hurried into the complex and saw Sgt. David Johnson, who had his shotgun firmly positioned under his arm. He was advising our Lieutenant that Paul was inside the apartment, and each time they tried to get to him, the suspect unloaded a spray of bullets in their direction. My stomach knotted in an instant. Paul, the hunter, was now the prey.

As the S.W.A.T sped to the scene, frantic pleas were yelled in order to assist Paul. I stood just outside the apartment building, and listened helplessly as muffled shots echoed inside from the suspect's gun. Finally, Sgt. Robert Moore was able to break into the apartment. The suspect refused to surrender and aimed his pistol directly at Sgt. Moore. A couple of quick shotgun blasts followed, and the suspect's life ended. Moments later, the apartment was cleared and several paramedics entered, carrying Paul out on a stretcher. He appeared unconscious as he passed me, blood on the side of his head and his usually neat hair in disarray. His color looked good, I tried to reassure myself, as the paramedics began CPR on him.

Several hours later, after the necessary paperwork was completed, I drove by Memorial Hospital. As I walked towards the Emergency Room entrance, I asked one of the attending officers how Paul was doing.

"We're waiting on the funeral home," he softly replied.

For the first time, I realized that Paul was gone.

I wasn't aware of the suspect's identity until hearing the press conference that afternoon. Chief Turner identified him as Jeffrey Scott Swafford. I was surprised, since I had arrested

Swafford in 1992 on a warrant alleging he fired shots into a house during a drive-by shooting. Knowing that he had numerous other arrests since then, I assumed he was hibernating in prison.

Services for Officer Scurry were held May 21, 1996. At age 48, Paul had been a police officer for twenty-one years. The funeral home wasn't large enough to hold a fraction of the anticipated guests, so the services were held at the Madison Church of Christ, with both the auditorium and balcony filled to capacity. The memorial was a true tribute to a hero. When it was over, I strolled outside, barely able to contain my emotions. When I heard the piper start playing "Amazing Grace" on the bagpipes, I broke down, tears spilling from my heart and onto my face.

And once again, another piece of my own soul died, as so many times before.

I climbed into Officer Jerry Dobbins car to ride in the procession. All around us were cruisers with flashing blue lights. The official count was 578 cars stretching across an eight mile escort to Paul's final resting place. Police cars representing countless departments fell into formation as they paid their respects to a fallen comrade; I even noticed cruisers from as far away as the Illinois State Police. As we drove down the highway, numerous citizens lined the sidewalks, some carrying flags in a show of respect. It's during times like this you realize that the community at large, often times silent, does appreciate the efforts expended on their behalf from those who serve and protect.

When we pulled into Springhill Cemetery, I watched as additional cars continued to arrive for the next 30 minutes. The Chattanooga Police Department even sent their honor guard. They looked like Marines, complete in dress whites, as they proudly carried the American flag.

Before I knew it, the service was over, and a hero was laid to rest.

Paul, I'll miss your easy smile and cheerful attitude. I'll miss the way you were always happy to assist anyone who asked, with the infinite patience of someone who really cared. You were a fine human being, Paul; and our department was a little bit better because of you.

I'm proud to say that you were my friend.

About the Author

Born in 1959 in Chattanooga, TN, Scott Fielden makes his book publishing debut with *Music City Blues*.

While attending Putnam County Senior High School in Cookeville, TN, he was a news and sports reporter for the award-winning high school newspaper, *The Cavalier*.

He graduated from East Tennessee State University in Johnson City, TN in 1977 with a marketing/management degree. Soon afterwards, he co-wrote and produced *Slade Rockgrip's Searching For America,* a radio-comedy program which later evolved into a newspaper series. He has also written several business publications for companies specializing in sales and marketing.

Scott currently resides in Johnson City with his wife, Brenda, and their Border Collie, Lucky.